THE CANDLE OF VISION

MACMILLAN AND CO., Limited
LONDON · BOMBAY · CALCUTTA · MADRAS
MELBOURNE

THE MACMILLAN COMPANY
NEW YORK · BOSTON · CHICAGO
DALLAS · SAN FRANCISCO

THE MACMILLAN CO. OF CANADA, Ltd.
TORONTO

THE
CANDLE OF VISION

BY

A. E.

= [pseud]

"The spirit of man is the candle of the Lord."—PROVERBS.
"When his candle shined upon my head and by his light
I walked through darkness."—JOB.

MACMILLAN AND CO., LIMITED
ST. MARTIN'S STREET, LONDON
1928

PRINTED IN GREAT BRITAIN
BY R. & R. CLARK, LIMITED, EDINBURGH

TO

JAMES STEPHENS

BEST OF COMPANIONS

PREFACE

When I am in my room looking upon the walls I have painted I see there reflections of the personal life, but when I look through the windows I see a living nature and landscapes not painted by hands. So, too, when I meditate I feel in the images and thoughts which throng about me the reflections of personality, but there are also windows in the soul through which can be seen images created not by human but by the divine imagination. I have tried according to my capacity to report about the divine order and to discriminate between that which was self-begotten fantasy and that which came from a higher sphere. These retrospects and meditations are the efforts of an artist and poet to relate his own vision to the vision of the seers and writers of the sacred books, and to discover what element of truth lay in those imaginations.

A. E.

CONTENTS

RETROSPECT

I HAD travelled all day and was tired, but I could not rest by the hearth in the cottage on the hill. My heart was beating with too great an excitement. After my year in the city I felt like a child who wickedly stays from home through a long day, and who returns frightened and penitent at nightfall, wondering whether it will be received with forgiveness by its mother. Would the Mother of us all receive me again as one of her children? Would the winds with wandering voices be as before the evangelists of her love? Or would I feel like an outcast amid the mountains, the dark valleys and the shining lakes? I knew if benediction came how it would come. I would sit among the rocks with shut eyes, waiting humbly as one waits in the ante-chambers of the mighty, and if the invisible ones chose me as companion they would begin with a soft breathing of their intimacies, creeping on me with shadowy affection like children who steal nigh to the bowed head and suddenly whisper fondness in the ear before it has even heard a footfall. So I stole out of the cottage and over the dark ridges to the place of rocks, and sat down, and let the coolness of the night chill and still the fiery dust in the brain. I waited trembling for the faintest touch, the shyest breathing of the Everlasting within my soul, the sign of reception and forgiveness. I knew it would come. I could not so desire what was not my own, and what is our own we cannot lose. Desire is hidden identity. The darkness drew me heavenward. From the hill the plains beneath slipped away grown vast and vague, remote and still. I seemed alone with immensity, and there came at last that melting of the divine darkness into the life within me for which I prayed. Yes, I still belonged, however humbly, to the heavenly household. I was not outcast. Still, though by a thread fine as that by which a spider hangs from the rafters, my being was suspended from the habitations of eternity. I longed to throw my arms about the hills, to meet with kisses the lips of the seraph wind. I felt the gaiety of childhood springing up through weariness

and age, for to come into contact with that
which is eternally young is to have that childhood of the spirit it must attain ere it can be
moulded by the Magician of the Beautiful and
enter the House of Many Mansions.

I had not always this intimacy with nature.
I never felt a light in childhood which faded
in manhood into the common light of day,
nor do I believe that childhood is any nearer
than age to this being. If it were so what
would the spirit have to hope for after youth
was gone? I was not conscious in my boyhood of any heaven lying about me. I lived
in the city, and the hills from which aid was
to come to me were only a far flush of blue
on the horizon. Yet I was drawn to them,
and as years passed and legs grew longer I
came nearer and nearer until at last one day
I found myself on the green hillside. I came
to play with other boys, but years were yet
to pass before the familiar places grew strange
once more and the mountains dense with fiery
forms and awful as Sinai.

While the child is still in its mother's
arms it is nourished by her, yet it does not
know it is a mother which feeds it. It knows
later in whose bosom it has lain. As the
mother nourishes the body so the Mighty

Mother nourishes the soul. Yet there are
but few who pay reverence where reverence
is due, and that is because this benign deity
is like a mother who indulges the fancies of
her children. With some she imparts life to
their own thoughts. Others she endows with
the vision of her own heart. Even of these
last some love in silence, being afraid to speak
of the majesty which smiled on them, and
others deceived think with pride : "This
vision is my own."

I was like these last for a long time. I
was aged about sixteen or seventeen years,
when I, the slackest and least ideal of boys,
with my life already made dark by those
desires of body and heart with which we so
soon learn to taint our youth, became aware
of a mysterious life quickening within my
life. Looking back I know not of anything
in friendship, anything I had read, to call this
forth. It was, I thought, self-begotten. I
began to be astonished with myself, for,
walking along country roads, intense and
passionate imaginations of another world, of
an interior nature began to overpower me.
They were like strangers who suddenly enter
a house, who brush aside the doorkeeper,
and who will not be denied. Soon I knew

they were the rightful owners and heirs of the house of the body, and the doorkeeper was only one who was for a time in charge, who had neglected his duty, and who had pretended to ownership. The boy who existed before was an alien. He hid himself when the pilgrim of eternity took up his abode in the dwelling. Yet, whenever the true owner was absent, the sly creature reappeared and boasted himself as master once more.

That being from a distant country who took possession of the house began to speak in a language difficult to translate. I was tormented by limitations of understanding. Somewhere about me I knew there were comrades who were speaking to me, but I could not know what they said. As I walked in the evening down the lanes scented by the honeysuckle my senses were expectant of some unveiling about to take place, I felt that beings were looking in upon me out of the true home of man. They seemed to be saying to each other of us, "Soon they will awaken; soon they will come to us again," and for a moment I almost seemed to mix with their eternity. The tinted air glowed before me with intelligible significance like a face, a voice. The visible world became like a tapestry blown and stirred by winds behind it.   If it would but raise for an instant I knew I would be in Paradise.   Every form on that tapestry appeared to be the work of gods.   Every flower was a word, a thought.   The grass was speech ; the trees were speech ; the waters were speech ; the winds were speech.   They were the Army of the Voice marching on to conquest and dominion over the spirit ; and I listened with my whole being, and then these apparitions would fade away and I would be the mean and miserable boy once more.   So might one have felt who had been servant of the prophet, and had seen him go up in the fiery chariot, and the world had no more light or certitude in it with that passing.   I knew these visitations for what they were and named them truly in my fantasy, for writing then in the first verses of mine which still seem to me to be poetry, I said of the earth that we and all things were her dreams :

> She is rapt in dreams divine.
> As her clouds of beauty pass
> On our glowing hearts they shine,
> Mirrored there as in a glass.
>
> Earth, whose dreams are we and they,
> With her deep heart's gladness fills
> All our human lips can say
> Or the dawn-fired singer trills.

Yet such is human nature that I still felt vanity as if this vision was mine, and I acted like one who comes across the treasure-house of a king, and spends the treasure as if it were his own. We may indeed have a personal wisdom, but spiritual vision is not to speak of as ours any more than we can say at the rising of the sun : " This glory is mine." By the sudden uprising of such vanities in the midst of vision I was often outcast, and found myself in an instant like those warriors of Irish legend, who had come upon a lordly house and feasted there and slept, and when they woke they were on the barren hillside, and the Faed Fia was drawn about that lordly house. Yet though the imagination apprehended truly that this beauty was not mine, and hailed it by its heavenly name, for some years my heart was proud, for as the beauty sank into memory it seemed to become a personal possession, and I said " I imagined this " when I should humbly have said, " The curtain was a little lifted that I might see." But the day was to come when I could not deny the Mighty Mother the reverence due, when I was indeed to know by what being I had been nourished, and to be made sweet and mad as a lover with the consciousness of her intermingling spirit.

The sages of old found that at the close of intense meditation their being was drawn into union with that which they contemplated. All desire tends to bring about unity with the object adored, and this is no less true of spiritual and elemental than of bodily desire ; and I, with my imagination more and more drawn to adore an ideal nature, was tending to that vital contact in which what at first was apprehended in fantasy would become the most real of all things. When that certitude came I felt as Dante might have felt after conceiving of Beatrice close at his side and in the Happy World, if, after believing it a dream, half hoping that it might here-after be a reality, that beloved face before his imagination grew suddenly intense, vivid and splendidly shining, and he knew beyond all doubt that her spirit was truly in that form, and had descended to dwell in it, and would be with him for evermore. So did I feel one warm summer day lying idly on the hillside, not then thinking of anything but the sunlight, and how sweet it was to drowse there, when, suddenly, I felt a fiery heart throb, and knew it was personal and intimate, and started with every sense dilated and intent, and turned inwards, and I heard first a music as of bells going away, away into that wondrous underland whither, as legend relates, the Danaan gods withdrew ; and then the heart of the hills was opened to me, and I knew there was no hill for those who were there, and they were unconscious of the ponderous mountain piled above the palaces of light, and the winds were sparkling and diamond clear, yet full of colour as an opal, as they glittered through the valley, and I knew the Golden Age was all about me, and it was we who had been blind to it but that it had never passed away from the world

THE EARTH BREATH

AFTER that awakening earth began more and more to bewitch me, and to lure me to her heart with honied entreaty. I could not escape from it even in that busy office where I sat during week-days with little heaps of paper mounting up before me moment by frenzied moment. An interval of inactivity and I would be aware of that sweet eternal presence overshadowing me. I was an exile from living nature but she yet visited me. Her ambassadors were visions that made me part of themselves. Through the hot foetid air of the gaslit room I could see the feverish faces, the quick people flitting about, and hear the voices; and then room, faces and voices would be gone, and I would be living in the Mother's being in some pure, remote, elemental region of hers. Instead of the dingy office there would be a sky of rarest amethyst; a snow - cold bloom of cloud; high up in the divine wilderness, solitary, a star; all rapt, breathless and still; rapt the seraph princes of wind and wave and fire, for it was the hour when the King, an invisible presence, moved through His dominions and Nature knew and was hushed at the presence of her Lord. Once, suddenly, I found myself on some remote plain or steppe, and heard unearthly chimes pealing passionately from I know not what far steeples. The earth-breath streamed from the furrows to the glowing heavens. Overhead the birds flew round and round crying their incomprehensible cries, as if they were maddened, and knew not where to nestle, and had dreams of some more enraptured rest in a diviner home. I could see a ploughman lifting himself from his obscure toil and stand with lit eyes as if he too had been fire-smitten and was caught into heaven as I was, and knew for that moment he was a god. And then I would lapse out of vision and ecstasy, and hear the voices, and see again through the quivering of the hot air the feverish faces, and seem to myself to be cast out of the spirit. I could hardly bear after thinking of these things, for I felt I was trapped in some obscure hell. You, too, trapped with me,

dear kindly people, who never said a harsh
word to the forgetful boy. You, too, I
knew, had your revelations. I remember
one day how that clerk with wrinkled face,
blinking eyes and grizzly beard, who never
seemed, apart from his work, to have in-
terests other than his pipe and paper, surprised me by telling me that the previous
midnight he waked in his sleep, and some
self of him was striding to and fro in the
moonlight in an avenue mighty with gigantic
images ; and that dream self he had surprised
had seemed to himself unearthly in wisdom
and power. What had he done to be so
high in one sphere and so petty in another ?
Others I could tell of, too, who had their
moment of awe when the spirit made its
ancient claim on them. But none were so
happy or so unhappy as I was. I was happy
at times because the divine world which had
meant nothing to my childhood was becoming
a reality to manhood : and I knew it was
not a dream, for comrades in vision soon
came to me, they who could see as I saw,
and hear as I heard, and there were some
who had gone deeper into that being than I
have ever travelled. I was more miserable
than my work-a-day companions, because the

very intensity of vision made the recoil more
unendurable. It was an agony of darkness
and oblivion, wherein I seemed like those
who in nightmare are buried in caverns so
deep beneath the roots of the world that
there is no hope of escape, for the way out is
unknown, and the way to them is forgotten
by those who walk in light. In those black
hours the universe, a gigantic presence,
seemed at war with me. I was condemned,
I thought, to be this speck of minute life
because of some sin committed in remote
ages, I and those with me. We were all lost
children of the stars. Everything that suggested our high original being, a shaft of
glory from the far fire in the heavens spear-
ing the gloom of the office, the blue twilight
deepening through the panes until it was
rich with starry dust, the sunny clouds career-
ing high over the city, these things would
stir pangs of painful remembrance and my
eyes would suddenly grow blind and wet.
Sometimes, too, I would rebel and plot in
my obscurity, and remember moments when
the will in me seemed to be a titanic power,
and my spirit would brood upon ways of
escape and ascent to its native regions, as
those fallen angels in Milton's tremendous

narrative rose up from torture, and conspired to tear the throne from Him. And then all that would appear to me to be futile as a speck of dust trying to stay itself against the typhoon, and the last door would close upon me and leave me more hopeless than before.

THE SLAVE OF THE LAMP

BECAUSE I was a creature of many imaginings and of rapid alternations of mood out of all that there came to me assurance of a truth, of all truths most inspiring to one in despair in the Iron Age and lost amid the undergrowths of being. I became aware of a swift echo or response to my own moods in circumstance which had seemed hitherto immutable in its indifference. I found every intense imagination, every new adventure of the intellect endowed with magnetic power to attract to it its own kin. Will and desire were as the enchanter's wand of fable, and they drew to themselves their own affinities. Around a pure atom of crystal all the atoms of the element in solution gather, and in like manner one person after another emerged out of the mass, betraying their close affinity to my moods as they were engendered. I met these people seemingly by accident along

country roads, or I entered into conversation
with strangers and found they were intimates
of the spirit.   I could prophesy from the
uprising of new moods in myself that I,
without search, would soon meet people of a
certain character, and so I met them.   Even
inanimate things were under the sway of these
affinities.   They yielded up to me what they
had specially for my eyes.   I have glanced in
passing at a book left open by some one in a
library, and the words first seen thrilled me,
for they confirmed a knowledge lately attained
in vision.   At another time a book taken
down idly from a shelf opened at a sentence
quoted from a Upanishad, scriptures then to
me unknown, and this sent my heart flying
eastwards because it was the answer to a
spiritual problem I had been brooding over
an hour before.   It was hardly a week after
my first awakening that I began to meet those
who were to be my lifelong comrades on the
quest, and who were, like myself, in a boyhood troubled by the spirit.   I had just
attempted to write in verse when I met a boy
whose voice was soon to be the most beautiful
voice in Irish literature.   I sought none of
these out because I had heard of them and
surmised a kinship.   The concurrence of our

personalities seemed mysterious and controlled by some law of spiritual gravitation, like that which in the chemistry of nature makes one molecule fly to another. I remember the exultation with which I realised about life that, as Heraclitus has said, it was in a flux, and that in all its flowings there was meaning and law ; that I could not lose what was my own ; I need not seek, for what was my own would come to me ; if any passed it was because they were no longer mine. One buried in a dungeon for many years could not have hailed sunshine, the sweet-smelling earth, and the long hidden infinitude of the skies more joyously than I the melting of that which had seemed immutable. It is those who live and grow swiftly, and who continually compare what is without with what is within, who have this certainty. Those who do not change see no change and recognise no law. He who has followed even in secrecy many lights of the spirit can see one by one the answering torches gleam. When I was made certain about this I accepted what befell with resignation. I knew that all I met was part of myself and that what I could not comprehend was related by affinity to some yet unrealised forces in my being. We have within us the Lamp of

c

the World ; and Nature, the genie, is Slave of
the Lamp, and must fashion life about us as
we fashion it within ourselves.   What we are
alone has power.   We may give up the outward personal struggle and ambition, and if
we leave all to the Law all that is rightly ours
will be paid.   Man becomes truly the Super-
man when he has this proud consciousness.
No matter where he may be, in what seeming
obscurity, he is still the King, still master of
his fate, and circumstance reels about him or
is still as he, in the solitude of his spirit, is
mighty or is humble.   We are indeed most
miserable when we dream we have no power
over circumstance, and I account it the
highest wisdom to know this of the living
universe that there is no destiny in it other
than that we make for ourselves.   How the
spirit is kindled, how it feels its power, when,
outwardly quiet, it can see the coming and
going of life, as it dilates within itself or
is still !   Then do we move in miracle and
wonder.   Then does the universe appear to
us as it did to the Indian sage who said that
to him who was perfect in meditation all rivers
were sacred as the Ganges and all speech
was holy.

MEDITATION

THERE is no personal virtue in me other than
this that I followed a path all may travel but
on which few do journey.   It is a path within
ourselves where the feet first falter in shadow
and darkness but which is later made gay by
heavenly light.   As one who has travelled a
little on that way and who has had some far-
off vision of the Many-Coloured Land, if I
tell what I know, and how I came to see most
clearly, I may give hope to those who would
fain believe in that world the seers spake of,
but who cannot understand the language
written by those who had seen that beauty of
old, or who may have thought the ancient
scriptures but a record of extravagant desires.
None need special gifts or genius.   Gifts !
There are no gifts.   For all that is ours we
have paid the price.   There is nothing we
aspire to for which we cannot barter some
spiritual merchandise of our own.   Genius !

There is no stinting of this by the Keeper of
the Treasure House. It is not bestowed but
is won. Yon man of heavy soul might if he
willed play on the lyre of Apollo, that drunkard
be god-intoxicated. Powers are not bestowed
by caprice on any. The formulae the chemist
illustrates, making exposition before his
students, are not more certainly verifiable
than the formulae of that alchemy by which
what is gross in us may be transmuted into
ethereal fires. Our religions make promises
to be fulfilled beyond the grave because they
have no knowledge now to be put to the test,
but the ancients spake of a divine vision to
be attained while we are yet in the body.
The religion which does not cry out : " I am
to-day verifiable as that water wets or that fire
burns. Test me that ye can become as gods."
Mistrust it. Its messengers are prophets of
the darkness. As we sink deeper into the
Iron Age we are met by the mighty devils of
state and empire lurking in the abyss, claiming
the soul for their own, moulding it to their
image, to be verily their own creature and not
heaven's. We need a power in ourselves
that can confront these mighty powers.
Though I am blind I have had moments of
sight. Though I have sinned I have been on

the path. Though I am feeble I have seen the way to power. I sought out ways to make more securely my own those magical lights that dawned and faded within me. I wished to evoke them at will and be master of my vision, and I was taught to do this which is as old as human life. Day after day, at times where none might interfere, and where none through love or other cause were allowed to interfere, I set myself to attain mastery over the will. I would choose some mental object, an abstraction of form, and strive to hold my mind fixed on it in un-wavering concentration, so that not for a moment, not for an instant, would the con-centration slacken. It is an exercise this, a training for higher adventures of the soul. It is no light labour. The ploughman's, cleaving the furrows, is easier by far. Five minutes of this effort will at first leave us trembling as at the close of a laborious day. It is then we realise how little of life has been our own, and how much a response to sensation, a drifting on the tide of desire. The rumour of revolt, the spirit would escape its thraldom, runs through the body. Empires do not send legions so swiftly to frustrate revolt as all that is mortal in us

hurries along nerve, artery, and every high-
way of the body to beset the soul. The
beautiful face of one we love, more alluring
than life, glows before us to enchant us from
our task. Old sins, enmities, vanities and
desires beleaguer and beseech us. If we do
not heed them then they change, they seem to
be with us, they open up vistas of all we and
they will do, when this new power we strive
for is attained. If we are tempted down that
vista we find with shame after an hour of
vain musing that we were lured away, had
deserted our task and forgotten that stern
fixity of the will we set out to achieve. Let
us persevere in our daily ritual and the
turmoil increases ; our whole being becomes
vitalised, the bad as well as the good. The
heat of this fervent concentration acts like
fire under a pot, and everything in our being
boils up madly. We learn our own hitherto
unknown character. We did not know we
could feel such fierce desires, never imagined
such passionate enmities as now awaken.
We have created in ourselves a centre of
power and grow real to ourselves. It is
dangerous, too, for we have flung ourselves
into the eternal conflict between spirit and
matter, and find ourselves where the battle is

hottest, where the foemen are locked in a death struggle. We are in grips with mightier powers than we had before conceived of. What man is there who thinks he has self-control? He stands in the shallow waters, nor has gone into the great deep, nor been tossed at the mercy of the waves. Let him rouse the arcane powers in himself, and he will feel like one who has let loose the avalanche. None would live through that turmoil if the will were the only power in ourselves we could invoke, for the will is neither good nor bad but is power only, and it vitalises good or bad indifferently. If that were all our labour would bring us, not closer to divine being, but only to a dilation of the personality. But the ancients who taught us to gain this intensity taught it but as preliminary to a meditation which would not waver and would be full of power. The meditation they urged on us has been explained as " the inexpressible yearning of the inner man to go out into the infinite." But that Infinite we would enter is living. It is the ultimate being of us. Meditation is a fiery brooding on that majestical Self. We imagine ourselves into Its vastness. We conceive ourselves as mirroring Its infinitudes, as moving in all things, as living in all beings, in earth, water, air, fire, æther. We try to know as It knows, to live as It lives, to be compassionate as It is compassionate. We equal ourselves to It that we may understand It and become It. We do not kneel to It as slaves, but as Children of the King we lift ourselves up to that Glory, and affirm to ourselves that we are what we imagine. "What a man thinks, that he is: that is the old secret," said the wise. We have imagined ourselves into this pitiful dream of life. By imagination and will we re-enter true being, becoming that we conceive of. On that path of fiery brooding I entered. At first all was stupor. I felt as one who steps out of day into the colourless night of a cavern, and that was because I had suddenly reversed the habitual motions of life. We live normally seeing through the eyes, hearing through the ears, stirred by the senses, moved by bodily powers, and receiving only such spiritual knowledge as may pass through a momentary purity of our being. On the mystic path we create our own light, and at first we struggle blind and baffled, seeing nothing, hearing nothing, unable to think, unable to imagine. We seem deserted by dream, vision or in-

spiration, and our meditation barren altogether. But let us persist through weeks or
months, and sooner or later that stupor disappears. Our faculties readjust themselves,
and do the work we will them to do.
Never did they do their work so well. The
dark caverns of the brain begin to grow
luminous. We are creating our own light.
By heat of will and aspiration we are trans-
muting what is gross in the subtle æthers
through which the mind works. As the
dark bar of metal begins to glow, at
first redly, and then at white heat, or as ice
melts and is alternately fluid, vapour, gas,
and at last a radiant energy, so do these
æthers become purified and alchemically
changed into luminous essences, and they
make a new vesture for the soul, and link us
to mid-world or heavenward where they too
have their true home. How quick the mind
is now! How vivid is the imagination!
We are lifted above the tumult of the body.
The heat of the blood disappears below us.
We draw nigher to ourselves. The heart
longs for the hour of meditation and hurries
to it ; and, when it comes, we rise within ourselves as a diver too long under seas rises
to breathe the air, to see the light. We have

invoked the God and we are answered according to old promise. As our aspiration so is our inspiration. We imagine It as Love and what a love enfolds us. We conceive of It as Might and we take power from that Majesty. We dream of It as Beauty and the Magician of the Beautiful appears everywhere at Its miraculous art, and the multitudinous lovely creatures of Its thought are busy moulding nature and life in their image, and all are hurrying, hurrying to the Golden World. This vision brings its own proof to the spirit, but words cannot declare or explain it. We must go back to lower levels and turn to that which has form from that which is bodiless.

THE MANY-COLOURED LAND

I HAVE always been curious about the psychology of my own vision as desirous of imparting it, and I wish in this book to relate the efforts of an artist and poet to discover what truth lay in his own imaginations. I have brooded longer over the nature of imagination than I have lingered over the canvas where I tried to rebuild my vision. Spiritual moods are difficult to express and cannot be argued over, but the workings of imagination may well be spoken of, and need precise and minute investigation. I surmise from my reading of the psychologists who treat of this that they themselves were without this faculty and spoke of it as blind men who would fain draw although without vision. We are overcome when we read *Prometheus Unbound*, but who, as he reads, flings off the enchantment to ponder in what state was the soul of Shelley in that ecstasy of swift

27

creation.   Who has questioned the artist to
whom the forms of his thought are vivid as
the forms of nature ?   Artist and poet have
rarely been curious about the processes of their
own minds.   Yet it is reasonable to assume
that the highest ecstasy and vision are
conditioned by law and attainable by all, and
this might be argued as of more importance
even than the message of the seers.   I attribute
to that unwavering meditation and fiery concentration of will a growing luminousness in
my brain as if I had unsealed in the body a
fountain of interior light.   Normally we close
our eyes on a cloudy gloom through which
vague forms struggle sometimes into definite-
ness.   But the luminous quality gradually
became normal in me, and at times in meditation there broke in on me an almost intolerable
lustre of light, pure and shining faces, dazzling
processions of figures, most ancient, ancient
places and peoples, and landscapes lovely as
the lost Eden.   These appeared at first to
have no more relation to myself than images
from a street without one sees reflected in a
glass ; but at times meditation prolonged
itself into spheres which were radiant with
actuality.   Once, drawn by some inner impulse
to meditate at an unusual hour, I found quick

oblivion of the body. The blood and heat of the brain ebbed from me as an island fades in the mists behind a swift vessel fleeting into light. The ways were open within. I rose through myself and suddenly felt as if I had awakened from dream. Where was I? In what city? Here were hills crowned with glittering temples, and the ways, so far as I could see, were thronged with most beautiful people, swaying as if shaken by some ecstasy running through all as if the Dark Hidden Father was breathing rapturous life within His children. Did I wear to them an aspect like their own? Was I visible to them as a new-comer in their land of lovely light? I could not know, but those nigh me flowed towards me with outstretched hands. I saw eyes with a beautiful flame of love in them looking into mine. But I could stay no longer for something below drew me down and I was again an exile from light.

There came through meditation a more powerful orientation of my being as if to a hidden sun, and my thoughts turned more and more to the spiritual life of Earth. All the needles of being pointed to it. I felt instinctively that all I saw in vision was part of the life of Earth which is a court where there

are many starry palaces.   There the Planetary
Spirit was King, and that Spirit manifesting
through the substance of Earth, the Mighty
Mother, was, I felt, the being I groped after
as God.   The love I had for nature as
garment of that deity grew deeper.   That
which was my own came to me as it comes to
all men.   That which claimed me drew me to
itself.   I had my days and nights of freedom.
How often did I start in the sunshine of a
Sabbath morning, setting my face to the hills,
feeling somewhat uncertain as a lover who
draws nigh to a beauty he adores, who sometimes will yield everything to him and
sometimes is silent and will only endure his
presence.   I did not know what would happen
to me, but I was always expectant, and walked
up to the mountains as to the throne of God.
Step by step there fell from me the passions
and fears of the week-day, until, as I reached
the hillside and lay on the grassy slope with
shut eyes, I was bare of all but desire for the
Eternal.   I was once more the child close to
the Mother.   She rewarded me by lifting for
me a little the veil which hides her true face.
To those high souls who know their kinship
the veil is lifted, her face is revealed, and
her face is like a bride's.   Petty as was my

everyday life, with the fears and timidities which abnormal sensitiveness begets, in those moments of vision I understood instinctively the high mood they must keep who would walk with the highest ; and who with that divine face glimmering before him could do aught but adore !

There is an instinct which stills the lips which would speak of mysteries whose day for revelation has not drawn nigh. The little I know of these I shall not speak of. It is always lawful to speak of that higher wisdom which relates our spiritual being to that multitudinous unity which is God and Nature and Man. The only justification for speech from me, rather than from others whose knowledge is more profound, is that the matching of words to thoughts is an art I have practised more. What I say may convey more of truth, as the skilled artist, painting a scene which he views for the first time, may yet suggest more beauty and enchantment than the habitual dweller, unskilled in art, who may yet know the valley he loves so intimately that he could walk blindfold from end to end.

I do not wish to write a book of wonders, but rather to bring thought back to that Being whom the ancient seers worshipped as Deity. I believe that most of what was said of God was in reality said of that Spirit whose body is Earth. I must in some fashion indicate the nature of the visions which led me to believe with Plato that the earth is not at all what the geographers suppose it to be, and that we live like frogs at the bottom of a marsh knowing nothing of that Many-Coloured Earth which is superior to this we know, yet related to it as soul to body. On that Many-Coloured Earth, he tells us, live a divine folk, and there are temples wherein the gods do truly dwell, and I wish to convey, so far as words may, how some apparitions of that ancient beauty came to me in wood or on hillside or by the shores of the western sea.

Sometimes lying on the hillside with the eyes of the body shut as in sleep I could see valleys and hills, lustrous as a jewel, where all was self-shining, the colours brighter and purer, yet making a softer harmony together than the colours of the world I know. The winds sparkled as they blew hither and thither, yet far distances were clear through that glowing air. What was far off was precise as what was near, and the will to see hurried me to what I desired. There, too, in that land I saw fountains as of luminous mist jetting from some hidden heart of power, and shining folk who passed into those fountains inhaled them and drew life from the magical air. They were, I believe, those who in the ancient world gave birth to legends of nymph and dryad. Their perfectness was like the perfectness of a flower, a beauty which had never, it seemed, been broken by act of the individualised will which with us makes possible a choice between good and evil, and the marring of the mould of natural beauty. More beautiful than we they yet seemed less than human, and I surmised I had more thoughts in a moment than they through many of their days. Sometimes I wondered had they individualised life at all, for they moved as if in some orchestration of their being. If one looked up, all looked up. If one moved to breathe the magical airs from the fountains, many bent in rhythm. I wondered were their thoughts all another's, one who lived within them, guardian or oversoul to their tribe ?

Like these were my first visions of super-nature, not spiritual nor of any high import, not in any way so high as those transcendental

D

moments of awe, when almost without vision
the Divine Darkness seemed to breathe within the spirit. But I was curious about these
forms, and often lured away by them from
the highest meditation ; for I was dazzled
like a child who escapes from a dark alley in
one of our cities of great sorrow where its
life has been spent, and who comes for the
first time upon some rich garden beyond the
city where the air is weighted with scent
of lilac or rose, and the eyes are made gay
with colour. Such a beauty begins to glow
on us as we journey towards Deity, even
as earth grows brighter as we journey from
the gloomy pole to lands of the sun ;
and I would cry out to our humanity,
sinking deeper into the Iron Age, that
the Golden World is all about us and that
beauty is open to all, and none are shut
out from it who will turn to it and seek
for it.

As the will grew more intense, the longing
for the ancestral self more passionate, there
came glimpses of more rapturous life in the
being of Earth. Once I lay on the sand
dunes by the western sea. The air seemed
filled with melody. The motion of the wind
made a continuous musical vibration. Now

and then the silvery sound of bells broke on my ear. I saw nothing for a time. Then there was an intensity of light before my eyes like the flashing of sunlight through a crystal. It widened like the opening of a gate and I saw the light was streaming from the heart of a glowing figure. Its body was pervaded with light as if sunfire rather than blood ran through its limbs. Light streams flowed from it. It moved over me along the winds, carrying a harp, and there was a circling of golden hair that swept across the strings. Birds flew about it, and over the brows was a fiery plumage as of wings of outspread flame. On the face was an ecstasy of beauty and immortal youth. There were others, a lordly folk, and they passed by on the wind as if they knew me not or the earth I lived on. When I came back to myself my own world seemed grey and devoid of light though the summer sun was hot upon the sands.

One other vision I will tell because it bears on things the ancients taught us, and on what I have to write in later pages. Where I saw this I will not say. There was a hall vaster than any cathedral, with pillars that seemed built out of living and trembling opal, or from some starry substances which shone with every colour, the colours of eve and dawn. A golden air glowed in this place, and high between the pillars were thrones which faded, glow by glow, to the end of the vast hall. On them sat the Divine Kings. They were fire-crested. I saw the crest of the dragon on one, and there was another plumed with brilliant fires that jetted forth like feathers of flame. They sat shining and starlike, mute as statues, more colossal than Egyptian images of their gods, and at the end of the hall was a higher throne on which sat one greater than the rest. A light like the sun glowed behind him. Below on the floor of the hall lay a dark figure as if in trance, and two of the Divine Kings made motions with their hands about it over head and body. I saw where their hands waved how sparkles of fire like the flashing of jewels broke out. There rose out of that dark body a figure as tall, as glorious, as shining as those seated on the thrones. As he woke to the hall he became aware of his divine kin, and he lifted up his hands in greeting. He had returned from his pilgrimage through darkness, but now an initiate, a master in the heavenly guild. While he gazed on them the tall golden figures from their thrones leaped up, they too with hands up-lifted in greeting, and they passed from me and faded swiftly in the great glory behind the throne.

ANALYTIC

BEFORE I may write more of that supernature which rises, a tower of heaven, above the depths where we move, I know I must try to solve some of the doubts and perplexities which come to most who hear of things they have not heard or seen for their own part. They will say, "You are an artist and have painted such things. We know you have imagination which creates images vividly. You are a poet, and it is the art of your tribe to gild for us the thoughts you have, the emotions you feel, so that what moods are common with us you attire richly till they walk like kings. But what certainty have you that it is not all fancy, and the visions you speak of were not born in the cloudy hollows of your brain, and are not glorified memories of things you have first seen with the sensual eye, and which were afterwards refashioned in memory ? What certitude have you that

38

these things you speak of are in any way
related to a real world invisible to our eyes ?"
To solve these doubts I must not fall back on
authority, or appeal for trust. It will avail
nothing to say that others have seen such
things and have with me looked upon them,
we speaking of them together as people who
see the same scene, who refer as they speak
to rocks, waters and trees, knowing these are
a common vision. It would be true if I said
this, but it would avail me nothing in my
desire that you should go hopefully on the
way I would have you journey. On that path,
as an ancient scripture says, to whatsoever
place one would travel that place one's own
self becomes, and I must try first to uproot
false ideas about memory, imagination and
vision so that by pure reason people may be
led out of error and be able to distinguish
between that which arises in themselves and
that which comes otherwise and which we
surmise is a visitor from a far country. I
too in boyhood had the idea so commonly
held that the pictures of imagination are old
memories refashioned. I first doubted this
as a child when, lying on my bed, there came
a sudden illumination of my brain, and pictures
moved before my inner eyes like the coloured

moving pictures we see in the theatre.   I saw,
I remember, a sunlit hillside which seemed
close to me.   There were huge grey boulders
strewn about.   Beyond this hill-slope I could
see far distant mountains, pale blue through
the sparkling air.   While I looked, giants in
brazen armour clambered swiftly up the hillside, swinging clubs which had spiked balls of
brass held by a chain at the end.   They
glittered in the sun as they ran up and past
me.   Motion, light, shadow, colour were
perfect as things seen passing before the
physical eyes.   Then the illumination in my
brain ceased, the picture vanished, and I was
startled, for I had seen no hillside like that,
no distant mountains, no giants in brazen
armour in picture or theatre, and I began a
speculation which soon ended because childhood keeps no prolonged meditation.   I may
take this as a type of vision common to most
people.   Either when they sit in darkness,
or with closed eyes, or as they drift into sleep
or awaken from sleep, they pass through
strange cities, float in the air, roam through
woods, have adventures with people who are
not the people they meet every day.   There
is nothing uncommon about such visions.
It is in the interpretation of them that error

arises. People pass them by too easily saying,
" It is imagination," as if imagination were
as easily explained as a problem in Euclid,
and was not a mystery, and as if every moving
picture in the brain did not need such minute
investigation as Darwin gave to earthworms.
I was asked to believe that giants, armour,
hillside and sunny distance so appeared in my
brain because I had seen men who might be
enlarged to giants, pictures of armour with
which they could be clothed by fancy, brass
with which the armour could be coloured.
Any rocks might be multiplied and enlarged
from memory by imagination to form a hillside,
and any sky of sunny blue would make my
distance. How plausible for a second ! How
unthinkable after a momentary consideration !
I know I could hardly, if you gave me a
hundred thousand pictures of heads, by cutting
them up and pasting them together, make a
fresh face which would appear authentic in
its tints and shadows, and it would be a work
of infinite labour. But these faces of vision
are not still. They move. They have life
and expression. The sunlight casts authentic
moving shadows on the ground. What is
it combines with such miraculous skill the
things seen, taking a tint here, a fragment of

form there, which uses the colours and forms
of memory as a palette to paint such master-
pieces ?   It has been said, " Every man is a
Shakespeare in his dreams."   The dreamer of
landscape is more than a Turner, because he
makes his trees to bend before the wind and
his clouds to fleet across the sky.   The waking
brain does not do this.   It is unconscious of
creation.   To say we refashion memories is
to surmise in the subconscious nature a
marvellous artist, to whom all that we have
ever seen with the physical eyes is present at
once, and as clay in the hands of a divine
potter, and it is such swift creation too that
it rivals the works of the Lord.   Well, I am
not one of those who deny that the Kingdom
of Heaven is within us or that the King is
also in His Heaven.   We need not deny that
and yet hold that vision comes otherwise.
Nor can be it denied that vision is often so
radiant and precise, for experience affirms that
it is, and hundreds of artists, and indeed
people who are not artists at all, will tell you
how clearly they see in their dreams.   But
for those who hold that visions such as I and
many others have had are only the refashioning
of memory, and there is nothing mysterious
about them, I say try to think out tint by

tint, form by form, how these could be recombined, and, for whatever marvel I would have you believe, you will have substituted something just as marvellous but not so credible. Not that it is incredible to think that the spirit in man is Creator, for all the prophets and seers of the world have told us that, but the common psychological explanation is not acceptable, because we know that forms can appear in the brain which were transferred by will from one person to another. When we know that, when we know this inner eye can see the form in another's mind, we must regard it as indicating an immense possibility of vision on that plane. We then ask ourselves concerning all these strange cities and landscapes of dream, all these impish faces which flout at us when we are drowsy, all these visions living and moving in our minds, whether they too came, not by way of the physical senses transformed in memory, but came like the image thought transferred, or by obscure ways reflected from spheres above us, from the lives of others and the visions of others. If we brood on this we will come to think the old explanation is untenable and will address ourselves with wonder and hope to the exploration of this strange country within ourselves, and will try to find out its limits, and whether from image or vision long pondered over we may not reach to their original being.

I think few of our psychologists have had imagination themselves. They have busy brains, and, as an Eastern proverb says, "The broken water surface reflects only broken images." They see too feebly to make what they see a wonder to themselves. They discuss the mode of imagination as people might discuss art, who had never seen painting or sculpture. One writer talks about light being a vibration, and the vibration affecting the eye and passing along the nerves until it is stored up in the brain cells. The vibration is, it appears, stayed or fixed there. Yet I know that every movement of mine, the words I speak, the circulation of my blood, cause every molecule in my body to vibrate. How is this vibration in the cells unaffected? It must remain unaffected in their hypothesis, for I can recall the original scene, can discuss it, can after years re-summon it again and find the image clear as at first. I refer to it in thought and it remains unchanged. The physical explanation of memory itself breaks down even as

the material explanation of imagination breaks
down. Can an unchanging vibration be retained when the substance which holds the
vibration is itself subject to continual movement? The moment we close our eyes and
are alone with our thoughts and the pictures
of dream, we are alone with mystery and
miracle. Or are we alone? Are we secure
there from intrusion? Are we not nearer
the thronged highways of existence where
gods, demons, men and goblins all are
psychical visitors. I will not speak here of
high things because I am trying to argue
with people who see no wonder in anything,
and dismiss all high things with a silly
phrase as fancy or imagination or hallucina-
tion. But I know from questioning many
people that it is common with them
before they sleep to see faces, while their
eyes are closed, and they are, as they think,
alone. These faces are sometimes the faces
of imps who frown at them, put out their
tongues at them, grin or gibber. Sometimes
not a face but a figure, or figures, will be
seen which, like the faces, seem endowed with
life. To call this imagination or fancy is
to explain nothing because the explanation is
not explained. The more one concentrates

on these most trivial mental apparitions, the more certain do we feel they have a life of their own, and that our brain is as full of living creatures as our body is thronged with tiny cells, each a life, or as the blood may swarm with bacteria. I draw attention to the mystery in obvious and common things, and ask that they be explained and not slurred over as if no explanation were necessary. I ask the doubters of my vision to penetrate a little into the mystery of their own thoughts and dreams before they cry out against me, who for many years travelled far and came upon lovely and inhabited regions to which I would also lead them. I know that my brain is a court where many living creatures throng, and I am never alone in it. You, too, can know that if you heighten the imagination and intensify the will. The darkness in you will begin to glow, and you will see clearly, and you will know that what you thought was but a mosaic of memories is rather the froth of a gigantic ocean of life, breaking on the shores of matter, casting up its own flotsam to mingle with the life of the shores it breaks on. If you will light your lamp you can gaze far over that ocean and even embark on it. Sitting in your chair

you can travel farther than ever Columbus
travelled and to lordlier worlds than his eyes
had rested on.   Are you not tired of surfaces ?   Come with me and we will bathe in
the Fountains of Youth.   I can point you
the way to El Dorado.

THE MINGLING OF NATURES

To move a single step we must have power.
To see we must be exalted. Not to be lost
in vision we must learn the geography of the
spirit and the many mansions in the being of
the Father. If we concentrate we shall have
power. If we meditate we shall lift ourselves
above the dark environment of the brain.
The inner shall become richer and more
magical to us than the outer which has held
us so long. How may I allure to this
meditation those who see only by the light
of day ; who, when their eyes are shut, are
as cave-dwellers living in a blackness beneath
the hills ? The cave of the body can be lit
up. If we explore it we shall there find
lights by which the lights of day are made
dim. I perhaps to build on had some little
gift of imagination I brought with me into
the world, but I know others who had no
natural vision who acquired this, and by

sustained meditation and by focussing the will to a burning-point, were raised above the narrow life of the body. Being an artist and a lover of visible beauty, I was often tempted from the highest meditation to contemplate, not divine being, but the mirage of forms. Yet because I was so bewitched and was curious about all I saw, I was made certain that the images which populate the brain have not always been there, nor are refashioned from things seen. I know that with the pictures of memory mingle pictures which come to us, sometimes from the minds of others, sometimes are glimpses of distant countries, sometimes are reflections of happenings in regions invisible to the outer eyes ; and as meditation grows more exalted, the forms traceable to memory tend to disappear and we have access to a memory greater than our own, the treasure-house of august memories in the innumerable being of Earth. When minute analysis is made of images in the brain, those foolish fables about memory and imagination no longer affect those who begin this quest, and we see how many streams are tributary to our life. All I have said may be proved by any as curious about things of the mind

E

as I was, if they will but light the candle on
their forehead and examine the denizens in
the brain. They will find that their sphere
is populous with the innermost thoughts of
others, and will more and more be led by
wonder and awe to believe that we and all
things swim in an æther of deity, and that
the least motion of our minds is incomprehensible except in memory of this : " In
Him we live and move and have our being."
Analysis of the simplest mental apparition
will lead us often to stay ourselves on that
thought.   Once in an idle interval in my
work I sat with my face pressed in my hands,
and in that dimness pictures began flickering
in my brain. I saw a little dark shop, the
counter before me, and behind it an old man
fumbling with some papers, a man so old
that his motions had lost swiftness and precision.   Deeper in the store was a girl, red-
haired, with grey watchful eyes fixed on the
old man.   I saw that to enter the shop one
must take two steps downwards from a
cobbled pavement without.   I questioned
a young man, my office companion, who
then was writing a letter, and I found that
what I had seen was his father's shop.
All my imaginations—the old man, his

yellow-white beard, his fumbling movements, the watchful girl, her colour, the steps, the cobbled pavement—were not imaginations of mine in any true sense, for while I was in a vacant mood my companion had been thinking of his home, and his brain was populous with quickened memories, and they invaded my own mind, and when I made question I found their origin. But how many thousand times are we invaded by such images and there is no speculation over them? Possibly I might have made use of such things in my art. I might have made a tale about the old man and girl. But if I had done so, if other characters had appeared in my tale who seemed just as living, where would they have come from? Would I have again been drawing upon the reservoir of my companion's memories? The vision of the girl and old man may in reality have been but a little part of the images with which my brain was flooded. Did I then see all, or might not other images in the same series emerge at some later time and the connection be lost? If I had written a tale and had imagined an inner room, an old mother, an absent son, a family trouble, might I not all the while be still adventuring in another's life? While we think we are imagining a character we may, so marvellous are the hidden ways, be really interpreting a being actually existing, brought into psychic contact with us by some affinity of sentiment or soul.

I brooded once upon a friend not then knowing where he was, and soon I seemed to myself to be walking in the night. Nigh me was the Sphinx, and, more remote, a dim pyramid. Months later my friend came to Ireland. I found he had been in Egypt at the time I had thought of him. He could not recollect the precise day, but had while there spent a night beside the great monuments. I did not see him in vision, but I seemed to be walking there in the night. Why did the angle of vision change as with one moving about ? Did I see through his eyes ? Or did I see, as in the other incident, images reflected from his sphere to my own ? Where does this vision end ? What are its limitations ? Would we, fully come to ourselves, be like those beings in the Apocalypse full of eyes within and without ? Would we, in the fulness of power, act through many men and speak through many voices ? Were Shakespeare and the great masters unconscious magi, blind visionaries, feeling and comprehending a life they could not see, or who, if they saw, thought it was their own creation. We must ask ourselves these questions, for, when our lamp is lit, we find the house of our being has many chambers, and creatures live there who come and go, and we must ask whether they have the right to be in our house ; and there are corridors there leading into the hearts of others, and windows which open into eternity, and we hardly can tell where our own being ends and another begins, or if there is any end to our being. If we brood with love upon this myriad unity, following the meditation ordained by Buddha for the brothers of his order, to let our minds pervade the whole wide world with heart of love, we come more and more to permeate, or to be pervaded by the lives of others. We are haunted by unknown comrades in many moods, whose naked souls pass through ours, and reveal themselves to us in an unforgettable instant, and we know them as we hardly know those who are the daily comrades of our heart, who, however intimate, are hidden from us by the husk of the body. As the inner life grows richer we beget more of these affinities. We wonder what relation

with them is rightly ours. Do we affect
them by a sympathy unknown to them as
they move us by a revelation more intimate
than could be uttered by words ? We discover in ourselves a new sense. By touch
with the soul we understand. We realise
how profound was that ancient wisdom
which told us when we were perfected in
concentration we could gain full comprehension of anything we wished by intent
brooding. I never attained that perfectness
of concentration, but I saw the possibilities
in moments of electric intensity of will when
I summoned out of the past a knowledge I
desired. How is this knowledge possible ?
Is there a centre within us through which all
the threads of the universe are drawn, a
spiritual atom which mirrors the spiritual
infinitudes even as the eye is a mirror of
the external heavens ? There is not a pin
point in visible space which does not contain
a microcosm of heaven and earth. We
know that, for nowhere do we move where
the eye does not receive its vision of infinity.
Is it only in the visible world, this condensation of the infinite in the atomic, and not
also in the soul and again in the spirit ?
What would the soul in its perfection mirror ?

Would it reflect within itself the myriad life
of humanity ? Would the spirit mirror the
heavens, and the imaginations of the Divine
Mind well up within it in mystic and transcendental ideations ? Or do they already
mirror each their own world, and is all knowledge already within us, and is our need
but for wisdom to create the links between
portions of a single being, dramatically
sundered by illusion as the soul is in dream ?
Is not the gathering of the will and the fiery
brooding to this end, and are the glimpses
we get of supernature caused but by the
momentary uplifting of an eye, by which,
when it is fully awakened, we dead shall be
raised ?

THE MEMORY OF EARTH

We experience the romance and delight of
voyaging upon uncharted seas when the
imagination is released from the foolish notion
that the images seen in reverie and dream are
merely the images of memory refashioned ;
and in tracking to their originals the forms
seen in vision we discover for them a varied
ancestry, as that some come from the minds
of others, and of some we cannot surmise
another origin than that they are portions of
the memory of Earth which is accessible to
us. We soon grow to think our memory
but a portion of that eternal memory and
that we in our lives are gathering an innumerable experience for a mightier being than our
own. The more vividly we see with the
inner eye the more swiftly do we come to
this conviction. Those who see vaguely are
satisfied with vague explanations which those
who see vividly at once reject as inadequate.

How are we to explain what has happened to many, and oftentimes to myself, that when we sit amid ancient ruins or in old houses they renew their life for us ? I waited for a friend inside a ruined chapel and while there a phantasm of its ancient uses came vividly before me. In front of the altar I saw a little crowd kneeling, most prominent a woman in a red robe, all pious and emotionally intent. A man stood behind these leaning by the wall as if too proud to kneel. An old man in ecclesiastical robes, abbot or bishop, stood, a crozier in one hand, while the other was uplifted in blessing or in emphasis of his words. Behind the cleric a boy carried a vessel, and the lad's face was vain with self-importance. I saw all this suddenly as if I was contemporary and was elder in the world by many centuries. I could surmise the emotional abandon of the red-robed lady, the proud indifference of the man who stood with his head but slightly bent, the vanity of the young boy as servitor in the ceremony, just as in a church to-day we feel the varied mood of those present. Anything may cause such pictures to rise in vivid illumination before us, a sentence in a book, a word, or contact with some object. I have brooded over the grassy mounds which are all that remain of the duns in which our Gaelic ancestors lived, and they builded themselves up again for me so that I looked on what seemed an earlier civilisation, saw the people, noted their dresses, the colours of natural wool, saffron or blue, how rough like our own homespuns they were ; even such details were visible as that the men cut meat at table with knives and passed it to the lips with their fingers. This is not, I am convinced, what people call imagination, an interior creation in response to a natural curiosity about past ages. It is an act of vision, a perception of images already existing breathed on some ethereal medium which in no way differs from the medium which holds for us our memories ; and the reperception of an image in memory which is personal to us in no way differs as a psychical act from the perception of images in the memory of Earth. The same power of seeing is turned upon things of the same character and substance. It is not only rocks and ruins which infect us with such visions. A word in a book when one is sensitive may do this also. I sought in a classical dictionary for information about some myth. What else on the page my eye caught I could not say, but something there made two thousand years to vanish. I was looking at the garden of a house in some ancient city. From the house into the garden fluttered two girls, one in purple and the other in a green robe, and they, in a dance of excitement, ran to the garden wall and looked beyond it to the right. There a street rose high to a hill where there was a pillared building. I could see through blinding sunlight a crowd swaying down the street drawing nigh the house, and the two girls were as excited as girls might be to-day if king or queen were entering their city. This instant uprising of images following a glance at a page cannot be explained as the refashioning of the pictures of memory. The time which elapsed after the page was closed and the apparition in the brain was a quarter of a minute or less. One can only surmise that pictures so vividly coloured, so full of motion and sparkle as are moving pictures in the theatres were not an instantaneous creation by some magical artist within us, but were evoked out of a vaster memory than the personal, that the Grecian names my eye had caught had the power of symbols which evoke their affinities, and the picture

of the excited girls and the shining procession
was in some fashion, I know not how, connected with what I had read. We cannot
pass by the uprising of these images with
some vague phrase about suggestion or
imagination and shirk further inquiry. If
with the physical eye twenty-five years ago a
man had seen a winged aeroplane amid the
clouds it had roused him to a tumult of
speculation and inquiry. But if the same
picture had been seen in the mind it would
speedily have been buried as mere fancy.
There would have been no speculation, though
what appears within us might well be deemed
more important than what appears without
us. Every tint, tone, shape, light or shade
in an interior image must have intelligible
cause as the wires, planes, engines and pro-
pellers of the aeroplane have. We must
infer, when the image is clear and precise,
an original of which this is the reflection.
Whence or when were the originals of the
pictures we see in dream or reverie ? There
must be originals ; and, if we are forced to
dismiss as unthinkable any process by which
the pictures of our personal memory could
unconsciously be reshaped into new pictures
which appear in themselves authentic copies

of originals, which move, have light, colour,
form, shade such as nature would bestow,
then we are led to believe that memory is an
attribute of all living creatures and of Earth
also, the greatest living creature we know,
and that she carries with her, and it is accessible to us, all her long history, cities far
gone behind time, empires which are dust, or
are buried with sunken continents beneath
the waters. The beauty for which men
perished is still shining ; Helen is there in
her Troy, and Deirdre wears the beauty which
blasted the Red Branch. No ancient lore
has perished. Earth retains for herself and
her children what her children might in
passion have destroyed, and it is still in the
realm of the Ever Living to be seen by
the mystic adventurer. We argue that this
memory must be universal, for there is nowhere we go where Earth does not breathe
fragments from her ancient story to the
meditative spirit. These memories gild the
desert air where once the proud and golden
races had been and had passed away, and they
haunt the rocks and mountains where the
Druids evoked their skiey and subterrene
deities. The laws by which this history is
made accessible to us seem to be the same as

those which make our own learning swift to our service. When we begin thought or discussion on some subject we soon find ourselves thronged with memories ready for use. Everything in us related by affinity to the central thought seems to be mobilised ; and in meditation those alien pictures we see, not the pictures of memory, but strange scenes, cities, beings and happenings, are, if we study them, all found to be in some relation to our mood. If our will is powerful enough and if by concentration and aspiration we have made the gloom in the brain to glow, we can evoke out of the memory of earth images of whatsoever we desire. These earth memories come to us in various ways. When we are passive, and the ethereal medium which is the keeper of such images, not broken up by thought, is like clear glass or calm water, then there is often a glowing of colour and form upon it, and there is what may be a reflection from some earth memory connected with the place we move in or it may be we have direct vision of that memory. Meditation again evokes images and pictures which are akin to its subject and our mood and serve in illustration of it. Once, when I was considering the play of arcane forces in the body, a book appeared before me, a coloured symbol on each page. I saw the book was magical, for while I looked on one of these the symbol vanished from the page, and the outline of a human body appeared, and then there came an interior revelation of that, and there was a shining of forces and a flashing of fires, rose, gold, azure and silver along the spinal column, and these flowed up into the brain where they struck upon a little ball that was like white sunfire for brilliancy, and they flashed out of that again in a pulsation as of wings on each side of the head ; and then the page darkened, and the changing series closed with the Caduceus of Mercury and contained only a symbol once more.

Such pictures come without conscious effort of will, but are clearly evoked by it. Lastly, but more rarely with me, because the electric intensity of will required was hard to attain, I was able at times to evoke deliberately out of the memory of nature pictures of persons or things long past in time, but of which I desired knowledge. I regret now, while I was young and my energies yet uncoiled, that I did not practise this art of evocation more in regard to matters where knowledge might be regarded as of spiritual value ; but I was like a child who discovers a whole set of fresh toys, and plays with one after the other, and I was interested in all that came to me, and was too often content to be the servant of my vision and not its master. It was an excitement of spirit for one born in a little country town in Ireland to find the circle of being widened so that life seemed to dilate into a paradise of beautiful memories, and to reach to past ages and to mix with the eternal consciousness of Earth, and when we come on what is new we pause to contemplate it, and do not hurry to the end of our journey. The instances of earth memories given here are trivial in themselves, and they are chosen, not because they are in any way wonderful, but rather because they are like things many people see, and so they may more readily follow my argument. The fact that Earth holds such memories is itself important, for once we discover this imperishable tablet, we are led to speculate whether in the future a training in seership might not lead to a revolution in human knowledge. It is a world where we may easily get lost, and spend hours in futile vision with no more gain than if one looked for long hours at the dust. For those to whom in their spiritual evolution these apparitions arise I would say : try to become the master of your vision, and seek for and evoke the greatest of earth memories, not those things which only satisfy curiosity, but those which uplift and inspire, and give us a vision of our own greatness ; and the noblest of all Earth's memories is the august ritual of the ancient mysteries, where the mortal, amid scenes of unimaginable grandeur, was disrobed of his mortality and made of the company of the gods.

F

IMAGINATION

In all I have related hitherto imagination was
not present but only vision. These are too
often referred to as identical, and in what I
have written I have tried to make clear the
distinction. If beyond my window I see
amid the manifolded hills a river winding
ablaze with light, nobody speaks of what is
seen as a thing imagined, and if I look out
of a window of the soul and see more marvels
of shining and shadow, neither is this an
act of imagination, which is indeed a higher
thing than vision, and a much rarer thing,
for in the act of imagination that which is
hidden in being, as the Son in the bosom of
the Father, is made manifest and a trans-
figuration takes place like that we imagine
in the Spirit when it willed, "Let there be
light." Imagination is not a vision of something which already exists, and which in
itself must be unchanged by the act of seeing,

but by imagination what exists in latency or essence is out-realised and is given a form in thought, and we can contemplate with full consciousness that which hitherto had been unrevealed, or only intuitionally surmised. In imagination there is a revelation of the self to the self, and a definite change in being, as there is in a vapour when a spark ignites it and it becomes an inflammation in the air. Here images appear in consciousness which we may refer definitely to an internal creator, with power to use or remould pre-existing forms, and endow them with life, motion and voice. We infer this because dream and vision sometimes assume a symbolic character and a significance which is personal to us. They tell us plainly, "For you only we exist," and we cannot conceive of what is seen as being a reflection of life in any sphere. In exploring the ancestry of the symbolic vision we draw nigh to that clouded majesty we divine in the depths of our being, and which is heard normally in intuition and conscience, but which now reveals character in its manifestation as the artist in his work. I had a gay adventure when I was a boy at the beginning of my mental travelling, when I met, not a lion, but a symbolic vision in

the path. I had read somewhere of one
whose dreams made a continuous story from
night to night, and I was excited at this and
wondered whether I too could not build up
life for myself in a fairyland of my own
creation, and be the lord of this in dream,
and offset the petty circumstance of daily life
with the beauty of a realm in which I would
be king. I bent myself to this, walking
about the country roads at night in the darkness, building up in fantasy the country of
sleep. I remember some of my gorgeous
fancies. My dream-world was self-shining.
Light was born in everything there at dawn,
and faded into a coloured gloom at eve, and
if I walked across my lawns in darkness the
grasses stirred by my feet would waken to
vivid colour and glimmer behind me in a
trail of green fire ; or if a bird was disturbed
at night in my shadowy woods it became a
winged jewel of blue, rose, gold and white,
and the leaves tipped by its wings would
blaze in flakes of emerald flame, and there
were flocks of wild birds that my shouts
would call forth to light with glittering
plumage the monstrous dusk of the heavens.
Many other fancies I had which I now forget,
and some of them were intuitions about the

Many-Coloured Land. After I had conceived this world, one night in a fury of
effort I willed that it should be my habita-
tion in dream. But of all my dreams I
remember only two. In the first I saw a
mass of pale clouds, and on them was
perched a little ape clutching at the misty
substance with its fingers and trying to
fashion it to some form. It looked from
its work every now and then at something beyond and below the clouds, and I
came closer in my dream and saw that
what the ape was watching was our earth
which spun below in space, and it was trying
to model a sphere of mist in mimicry of that
which spun past it. While I was intent, this
grotesque sculptor turned suddenly, looking
at me with an extraordinary grimace which
said clearly as words could say, "That is
what you are trying to do," and then I was
whirled away again and I was the tiniest
figure in vast mid-air, and before me was a
gigantic gate which seemed lofty as the skies,
and a shadowy figure filled the doorway and
barred my passage. That is all I can remember, and I am forced by dreams like this
to conclude there is a creator of such dreams
within us, for I cannot suppose that anywhere

in space or time a little ape sat on a cloud
and tried to fashion it into planetary form.
The creator of that vision was transcendent
to the waking self and to the self which
experienced the dream, for neither self took
conscious part in the creation. The creator
of that vision was seer into my consciousness
in waking and in sleep, for what of the vision
I remember was half a scorn of my effort and
half a warning that my ambition was against
natural law. The creator of that vision could
combine forms and endow them with motion
and life for the vision was intellectual and
penetrated me with its meaning. Is it ir-
rational to assume so much, or that the
vision indicated a peculiar character in its
creator, and that the ironic mood was not
alien to it nor even humour ? I am rather
thankful to surmise this of a self which waves
away so many of our dreams and joys, and
which seems in some moods to be remote
from the normal and terrible as the angel
with the flaming sword pointing every way
to guard the Tree of Life. In this dream
some self of me, higher in the tower of our
being which reaches up to the heavens, made
objective manifestations of its thought ; but
there were moments when it seemed itself to

descend, wrapping its memories of heaven about it like a cloth, and to enter the body, and I knew it as more truly myself than that which began in my mother's womb, and that it was antecedent to anything which had body in the world. Here I must return to those imaginations I had walking about the country roads as a boy, and select from these, as I have done from vision, things upon which the reason may be brought to bear. It is more difficult, for when there is divine visitation the mortal is made dark and blind with glory and, in its fiery fusion with the spirit, reason is abased or bewildered or spreads too feeble a net to capture Leviathan, for often we cannot after translate to ourselves in memory what the spirit said, though every faculty is eager to gather what is left after the visitation even as the rabble in eastern legend scramble to pick up the gold showered in the passing of the king. By the time I was seventeen or eighteen my brain began to flicker with vivid images. I tried to paint these, and began with much enthusiasm a series of pictures which were to illustrate the history of man from his birth in the Divine Mind where he glimmered first in the darkness of chaos in vague and monstrous forms growing ever nigher to the human, to men beasts and men birds, until at last the most perfect form, the divine idea of man, was born in space. I traced its descent into matter, its conflict with the elements, and finally the series ended in a pessimistic fancy where one of our descendants millions of years hence, a minute philosopher, a creature less than three inches in height, sat on one of our gigantic skulls and watched the skies ruining back into their original chaos and the stars falling from their thrones on the height. Most of these pictures were only the fancies of a boy, but in considering one of the series I began to feel myself in alliance with a deeper consciousness, and that was when I was trying to imagine the apparition in the Divine Mind of the idea of the Heavenly Man. Something ancient and eternal seemed to breathe through my fancies. I was blinded then by intensity of feeling to the demerits of the picture, but I was excited in an extraordinary way over what I had done, and I lay awake long into the night brooding over it. I asked myself what legend I would write under the picture. Something beyond reason held me, and I felt like one who is in a dark room and hears the breathing of another creature, and himself waits breathless for its utterance, and I struggled to understand what wished to be said, and at last, while I was preternaturally dilated and intent, something whispered to me, "Call it the Birth of Aeon." The word "Aeon" thrilled me, for it seemed to evoke by association of ideas, moods and memories most ancient, out of some ancestral life where they lay hidden ; and I think it was the following day that, still meditative and cling-ing to the word as a lover clings to the name of the beloved, a myth incarnated in me, the story of an Aeon, one of the first starry emanations of Deity, one pre-eminent in the highest heavens, so nigh to Deity and so high in pride that he would be not less than a god himself and would endure no dominion over him save the law of his own will. This Aeon of my imagination revolted against heaven and left its courts, descending into the depths where it mirrored itself in chaos, weaving out of the wild elements a mansion for its spirit. That mansion was our earth and that Aeon was the God of our world. This myth incarnated in me as a boy walking along the country roads in Armagh. I re-turned to Dublin after a fortnight and it was

a day or two after that I went into the Library
at Leinster House and asked for an art
journal.   I stood by a table while the attend-
ant searched for the volume.   There was a
book lying open there.   My eye rested on it.
It was a dictionary of religions, I think, for
the first word my eye caught was "Aeon"
and it was explained as a word used by the
Gnostics to designate the first created beings.
I trembled through my body.   At that time
I knew nothing of mystical literature and
indeed little of any literature except such tales
as a boy reads, and the imaginations which
had begun to overwhelm me were to me
then nothing but mere imaginations, and were
personal and unrelated in my mind with any
conception of truth, or idea that the imagination could lay hold of truth.   I trembled
because I was certain I had never heard the
word before, and there rushed into my mind
the thought of pre-existence and that this
was memory of the past.   I went away
hurriedly that I might think by myself, but
my thoughts drove me back again soon, and
I asked the librarian who were the Gnostics
and if there was a book which gave an account
of their ideas.   He referred me to a volume of
Neander's *Church History*, and there, in the

section dealing with the Sabaeans, I found the myth of the proud Aeon who mirrored himself in chaos and became the lord of our world. I believed then, and still believe, that the immortal in us has memory of all its wisdom, or, as Keats puts it in one of his letters, there is an ancestral wisdom in man and we can if we wish drink that old wine of heaven. This memory of the spirit is the real basis of imagination, and when it speaks to us we feel truly inspired and a mightier creature than ourselves speaks through us. I remember how pure, holy and beautiful these imaginations seemed, how they came like crystal water sweeping aside the muddy current of my life, and the astonishment I felt, I who was almost inarticulate, to find sentences which seemed noble and full of melody sounding in my brain as if another and greater than I had spoken them ; and how strange it was also a little later to write without effort verse, which some people still think has beauty, while I could hardly, because my reason had then no mastery over the materials of thought, pen a prose sentence intelligently. I am convinced that all poetry is, as Emerson said, first written in the heavens, that is, it is conceived by a self deeper than appears in normal life, and when it speaks to us or tells us its ancient story we taste of eternity and drink the Soma juice, the elixir of immortality.

DREAMS

I HAD discovered through such dreams as
that of the satirical ape that there is One
who is vigilant through the sleep of the
body, and I was led by other dreams to
assume that in the heart of sleep there is
an intellectual being moving in a world of
its own and using transcendental energies.
Most of the dreams we remember are
chaotic, and these seem often to be deter-
mined in character by the accident which
brings about our waking. Chaotic as these
are, they are full of wonder and miracle, for
in the space of a second, almost before a
voice has reached the ear of the sleeper
or a hand has touched him, some magical
engineer has flung a bridge of wild incident
over which the spirit races from deep own-
being unto outward being. Never when
awake could we pack into a second of vivid
imagination the myriad incidents that the

artificer of dream can create to bring us
from the being we remember not back to
the dream of life. This magical swiftness of
creation in dream has been noted by many,
and those who have had experience of even
the most nightmare happenings before waking must be led to surmise that within that
blankness we call sleep there is a consciousness in unsleeping vigilance, and this being,
which is unsleeping while the body sleeps,
excites us to a curiosity as wild as ever
led adventurer across uncharted seas. The
ancient seers made earth world, mid-world
and heaven world synonyms for three states
of consciousness, waking, dreaming and
deep sleep. But the dream state of the
soul moving in the mid-world of which they
spoke is an intellectual state, and its character
is not easily to be guessed from that chaos
of fancies we ordinarily remember and call
our dreams ; and which I think are not true
dreams at all but rather a transitional state
on the borderland, like to the froth on the
ocean fringes, where there are buffetings of
air, churnings of sand, water and weed,
while beyond is the pure deep. I had but
slight experience of that loftier life in dream
which to others I know was truer life than

waking. But none can speak truly of the dreams or imaginations of others, but only of what themselves have known. In intensest meditation I think we encroach on that state which to the waking brain is veiled by sleep and is normally a blank, for in the highest dreams of which I retained memory I was on a plane of being identical with that reached in the apex of meditation and had perceptions of a similar order of things. The black curtain of unconsciousness which drapes the chambers of the brain in sleep, once, for an instant, was magically lifted for me, and I had a glimpse of the high adventures of the unsleeping soul. I found myself floating on the luminous night in a body lighter than air and charged with power, buoyed up above a mountainous region. Beneath me was a wrinkled dusk like the crater of some huge volcano. There were others with me, people with airy glittering bodies, all, like myself, intent on a being mightier than our own. A breath of power poured upward from below as from a fountain, or as if from here some sidereal river flowed out to the country of the stars. We hovered over the fountain from which came that invisible breath filling us with delight and power. While we hung intent there came the apparition of a vast and glowing orb of light like the radiance about a god, and of those glittering ones some flung themselves into that sphere of light, and were absorbed in it : and it faded away, ebbing from us as if it had been a living galleon come to the hither side of being but for a moment, to carry with it those who might go to the heaven world to be partakers of the divine nature and live in their parent Flame. I could not cross with that Charon, and I remembered no more, for the curtain of darkness which was magically lifted was again dropped over the chambers of the brain. But when I woke I was murmuring to myself, as if in interpretation, the words of the Apostle, " We all with open face beholding as in a glass the glory of the Lord are changed unto the same image from glory to glory," and I knew there were many at that mystery who would wake up again outcasts of Heaven, and the God of this world would obliterate memory so that they would never know they had kept tryst with the Kabiri.

Once before, not in dream but in meditation, there had broken in upon me such a

light from the secret places; and I saw
through earth as through a transparency to
one of those centres of power, "fountains
out of Hecate" as they are called in the
Chaldaic oracles, and which are in the being
of earth, even as in ourselves there are fiery
centres undiscovered by the anatomist where
thought is born or the will leaps up in flame.
And then, and in the dream I have just told,
and in that other vision of the heavenly city
where I found myself among the shining
ones, there seemed to be little of personal
fantasy as there was in the dream of the
ape, but I seemed to myself to be moving
in a real nature which others also have
moved in, and which was perhaps the sphere
known also to that spiritual geographer who
assured Socrates of a many-coloured earth
above this with temples wherein the gods
do truly dwell. I do not wish now to urge
this but only to draw the deductions any
psychologist analysing dream might draw
from dreams not mystical in character. I
may liken myself in my perception of that
dream to a man in a dark hall so utterly
lightless, so soundless, that nothing reaches
him; and then the door is suddenly flung
open, and he sees a crowd hurrying by, and

G

then the door is closed and he is again in
darkness. Such a man seeing through the
door a procession of people in the streets
knows they had a life before they came nigh
the door and after they passed the door ;
and he is not foolish if he speculates on this
and how they gathered and for what purpose.
So I am justified, I think, in assuming that
there was some psychic action in priority to
my moment of consciousness. I must seek
intellectual causes for events which have
logical structure and coherency : I cannot
assume that that sudden consciousness of
being in the air was absolutely the beginning
of that episode any more than I can imagine
a flower suddenly appearing without plant or
root or prior growth ; nor can I think that
blind motions of the brain, in blank unconsciousness of what they tend to, suddenly
flame into a consciousness instinct with wild
beauty. To assume that would be a freak
in reasoning. I might with as much wisdom
assume that if in the darkness I took my
little son's box of alphabetical bricks, and
scattered them about blindly, when the light
was turned on I might find that the letters
composed a noble sentence. I can reason-
ably take either of two possibilities, one

being that the dream was self-created fantasy only, and the other that it was the mirroring in the brain of an experience of soul in a real sphere of being. But whether we assume one or other we postulate an unsleeping consciousness within ourselves while the brain is asleep : and that unsleeping creature was either the creator of the dream or the actor in a real event. Who is that unsleeping creature ? Is it the same being who daily inhabits the brain ? Does it rise up when the body sinks on the couch ? Has it a dual life as we have when waking, when half our consciousness is of an external nature and half of subjective emotions and thoughts ? Are part of our dreams internal fantasy and part perceptions of an external sphere of being ? If I assume that the soul was an actor in a real event which was mirrored in the brain, why did I remember only one moment of the adventure ? To see any being means that we are on the same plane. I see you who are physical because I also have bodily life. If I see an elemental being or a heavenly being it means that some part of me is on the same plane of being or substance. Had I by meditation and concentration evolved in myself

some element akin to that breathed upward
from the mystic fountain, and when the soul
inhaled this fiery essence a rapport began
between free soul and slumbering body, the
circuit was complete, and sleeping and unsleeping being became one ?   On that hypothesis there were journeyings of the soul
before and after the moment remembered,
but the action in priority and in succession I
could not remember because there was as
yet no kinship in the brain to the mood of
the unsleeping soul or to the deed it did.
If the soul is an actor in deep sleep, seeing,
hearing and moving in a world of real
energies, then we are justified in assuming a
psychic body within the physical, for to see,
to hear, to move are functions of an organism
however ethereal.   Is it the shining of the
Psyche we perceive within ourselves when
through aspiration the body becomes filled
with interior light and consciousness is
steeped in a brilliancy of many colours while
the eyes are closed ?   Are we then like the
half-evolved dragon-fly who catches with the
first cracking of its sheath a glimpse of its
own gorgeous plumage ?   Was it this body
the prophet spoke of when he said, "Thou
hast been in Eden the Garden of God :

every precious stone was thy covering . . .
thou wast upon the holy mountain of God :
thou hast walked up and down amid the
stones of fire ? "   And was this spiritual life
lost to man because his heart was lifted up
because of his beauty, and wisdom was cor-
rupted by reason of its own brightness ?

If we brood over the alternative that the
dream was self-begotten fantasy, no less
must we make obeisance to the dreamer of
dreams. Who is this who flashes on the
inner eye landscapes as living as those we
see in nature ? The winds blow cool upon
the body in dream : the dew is on the
grass : the clouds fleet over the sky : we
float in air and see all things from an angle
of vision of which on waking we have no
experience : we move in unknown cities and
hurry on secret missions. It matters not
whether our dream is a grotesque, the same
marvellous faculty of swift creation is in it.
We are astonished at nightmare happenings
no less than at the lordliest vision, for we
divine in the creation of both the same
magical power. I cannot but think the gnat
to be as marvellous as the Bird of Paradise,
and these twain no less marvellous than
the seraphim. The Master of Life is in all,

and I am as excited with wonder at the creative genius shown in the wildest dream as in the most exalted vision. Not by any power I understand are these images created : but the power which creates them is, I surmise, a mightier self of ours, and yet our slave for purposes of its own. I feel its presence in all I do, think or imagine. It waits on my will. It is in the instant and marvellous marshalling of memories when I speak or write. Out of the myriad chambers of the soul where they lie in latency, an hundred or a thousand memories rise up, words, deeds, happenings, trivial or mighty, the material for thought or speech waiting in due order for use. They sink back silently and are again ready : at the least desire of the will they fly up to consciousness more swiftly than iron filings to the magnet. If I am wakened suddenly I surmise again that it is that enchanter who builds miraculously a bridge of incident to carry me from deep being to outward being. When thought or imagination is present in me, ideas or images appear on the surface of consciousness, and though I call them my thoughts, my imaginations, they are already formed when I become aware of them. The Indian sage Sankara says by reason of the presence of the highest Self in us, the mind in us is moved as if moved by another than ourselves. Upon its presence depend all motions of body and soul. Could I embrace even the outer infinitude with the eye of the body, if it did not preside over the sense of sight, infinitude interpreting infinitude ? It seems to wait on us as indifferently and as swiftly when the will in us is evil as when it is good. It will conjure up for us images of animalism and lust at the call of desire. It might speak of itself as the Lord spoke of Himself to the prophet : "From me spring forth good and evil." But if we evoke it for evil it answers with fading power, and we soon are unable to evoke it for good, for the evil we have called forth works for our feebleness and extinction. Or is there another and evil genie, a dark effigy of the higher also waiting on us as slave of our desires? I do not know. Was it of the higher it was said, "Ask, and ye shall receive. Seek, and ye shall find. Knock, and it shall be opened to you"? Can we by searching find out its ways ? Can we come to an identity of ourselves with it ? Again I do not know, but the more I ponder over this unsleeping being, the more do I feel astonished as Aladdin with lamp or ring, who had but to touch the talisman and a legion of genii were ready to work his will, to build up for him marvellous palaces in the twinkling of an eye, and to ransack for him the treasure-houses of eternity.

THE ARCHITECTURE OF DREAM

I HAVE failed in my purpose if I have not made it clear that in the actual architecture of dream and vision there is a mystery which is not explained by speaking of suppressed desire or sex or any of those springs which modern psychologists surmise are released in dream. A mood may attract its affinities but it does not create what it attracts, and between anger and a definite vision of conflict there is a gulf as mysterious as there was between Aladdin's desire and the building of his marvellous palace. I desire a house, but desire does not build it. I design a house, but every line is drawn with full consciousness, and when I give the plan to the builder every brick is placed with full consciousness by the masons. No coherent architecture in city or dream arises magically by some unreason which translates bodiless desire into organic form. However

swift the succession may be, in that second
of time between desire and its visionary
embodiment or fulfilment there must be
space for intellectual labour, the construc-
tion of forms or the choice of forms, and
the endowing of them with motion.   A
second to my brain is too brief a fragment
of time for more than sight, but I must
believe that to a more intense consciousness,
which is co-worker with mine, that second
may suffice for a glimpse into some pleroma
of form for the selection of these and the
unrolling of a vast pageantry.   Something
there is, a creature within me, behind whose
swiftness I falter a hopeless laggard, for it
may be a traveller through the Archaeus and
back again with the merchandise of its travel
before my pulse has beaten twice.   As an
artist who has laboured slowly at the creation
of pictures I assert that the forms of dream
or vision if self-created require a conscious
artist to arrange them, a magician to endow
them with life, and that the process is
intellectual, that is, it is conscious on some
plane of being, though that self which sits
in the gate of the body does not know what
powers or dignitaries meet in the inner
palace chambers of the soul.   When we have

dreams of flying and see all things from an angle of vision of which we never could have experience in waking, we know that to speak of the moving pictures of dream as memories or unconscious recombinations of things seen when waking, is to speak without subtlety or intellectual comprehension. I criticise the figures I see in dream or vision exactly as I would the figures in a painting. Even if I see a figure in dream I have seen when waking, if the figure acts in a manner differing from its action when seen with the physical eye, if it now walks when it then sat, or looks down where before it looked up, and if these motions in dream appear authentic so that face and form have the proper light and shade and the anatomies are undistorted, that dream change in the figure of memory is itself a most perplexing thing. We must suppose that memory as memory is as fixed in its way as a sun - picture is fixed or as the attitude of a statue is fixed. If it fades it should be by loss of precision and not into other equally precise but different forms and gestures. Now we could not without cracks or distorting of anatomies or complete re-modelling change the pose of a statue even if it was modelled in some easily malleable substance ; and the plastic change from stillness to motion in a figure, which we presume to be a memory, is wonderful when we think of it, as wonderful as if the little Tanagra in clay upon my shelf should change from its cast solidity and walk up and down before me. For myself I think man is a protean being, within whose unity there is diversity, and there are creatures in the soul which can inform the images of our memory, or the eternal memory, aye, and speak through them to us in dream, so that we hear their voices, and it is with us in our minute microcosmic fashion even as it was said of the universe that it is a soliloquy of Deity wherein Ain-Soph talks to Ain-Soph.

We can make such general speculations about all pictures moving before the inner eye, and it is always worth while investigating the anatomy of vision and to be intent on what appears to us, for if we have intentness we have memory. A mental picture which at first had yielded nothing to us may be followed by others which indicate a relation to the earliest in the series so that they seem like pages read at different times from the

same book. When I was young I haunted
the mountains much, finding in the high air
vision became richer and more luminous. I
have there watched for hours shining landscape and figures in endless procession, trying
to discover in these some significance other
than mere beauty. Once on the hillside I
seemed to slip from to-day into some remote
yesterday of earth. There was the same
valley below me, but now it was deepening
into evening and the skies were towering up
through one blue heaven to another. There
was a battle in the valley and men reeled
darkly hither and thither. I remember one
warrior about whom the battle was thickest,
for a silver star flickered above his helmet
through the dusk. But this I soon forgot
for I was impelled to look upwards, and there
above me was an airship glittering with light
It halted above the valley while a man, grey-
bearded, very majestic, his robes all starred
and jewelled, bent over and looked down
upon the battle. The pause was but for an
instant, and then the lights flashed more
brilliantly, some luminous mist was jetted
upon the air from many tubes below the boat,
and it soared and passed beyond the mountain,
and it was followed by another and yet others,

all glittering with lights, and they climbed
the air over the hill and were soon lost amid
the other lights of heaven. It must be a
quarter of a century ago since I saw this vision
which I remember clearly because I painted
the ship, and it must, I think, be about five
or six years after that a second vision in the
same series startled me. I was again on the
high places, and this time the apparition in
the mystical air was so close that if I could
have stretched out a hand from this world to
that I could have clutched the aerial voyager
as it swept by me. A young man was steer-
ing the boat, his black hair blown back from
his brows, his face pale and resolute, his head
bent, his eyes intent on his wheel : and beside
him sat a woman, a rose-coloured shawl
speckled with golden threads drawn over her
head, around her shoulders, across her bosom
and folded arms. Her face was proud as a
queen's, and I long remembered that face for
its pride, stillness and beauty. I thought at
the moment it was some image in the eternal
memory of a civilisation more remote than
Atlantis and I cried out in my heart in a
passion of regret for romance passed away
from the world, not knowing that the world's
great age was again returning and that soon

we were to swim once more beneath the epic skies. After that at different times and places I saw other such aerial wanderers, and this I noted, that all such visions had a character in keeping with each other, that they were never mixed up with modernity, that they had the peculiarities by which we recognise civilisations as distinct from each other, Chinese from Greek or Egyptian from Hindu. They were the stuff out of which romance is made, and if I had been a story-teller like our great Standish O'Grady I might have made without questioning a wonder tale of the air, legendary or futurist, but I have always had as much of the philosophic as the artistic interest in what people call imagination, and I have thought that many artists and poets gave to art or romance what would have had an equal if not a greater interest as psychology. I began to ask myself where in the three times or in what realm of space these ships were launched. Was it ages ago in some actual workshop in an extinct civilisation, and were these but images in the eternal memory? Or were they launched by my own spirit from some magical arsenal of being, and, if so, with what intent? Or were they images of things yet to be in

the world, begotten in that eternal mind
where past, present and future coexist, and
from which they stray into the imagination
of scientist, engineer or poet to be out-realised
in discovery, mechanism or song ?   I find it
impossible to decide.   Sometimes I even
speculate on a world interpenetrating ours
where another sun is glowing, and other stars
are shining over other woods, mountains,
rivers and another race of beings.   And I
know not why it should not be so.   We are
forced into such speculations when we become
certain that no power in us of which we are
conscious is concerned in the creation of such
visionary forms.   If these ships were launched
so marvellously upon the visionary air by
some transcendent artisan of the spirit they
must have been built for some purpose and
for what ?   I was not an engineer intent on
aerial flight, but this is, I think, notable that at
the moment of vision I seemed to myself to
understand the mechanism of these airships,
and I felt, if I could have stepped out of this
century into that visionary barque, I could
have taken the wheel and steered it confidently on to its destiny.   I knew that the
closing of a tube at one side of the bow would
force the ship to steer in that direction,

because the force jetted from the parallel tube on the other side, no longer balanced by an equal emission of power, operated to bring about the change. There is an interest in speculating about this impression of knowledge for it might indicate some complicity of the subconscious mind with the vision which startled the eye. That knowledge may have been poured on the one while seeing was granted to the other. If the vision was imagination, that is if the airship was launched from my own spirit, I must have been in council with the architect, perhaps in deep sleep. If I suppose it was imagination I am justified in trying by every means to reach with full consciousness to the arsenal where such wonders are wrought. I cannot be content to accept it as imagination and not try to meet the architect. As for these visions of airships and for many others I have been unable to place them even speculatively in any world or any century, and it must be so with the imaginations of many other people. But I think that when we begin speculation about these things it is the beginning of our wakening from the dream of life.

I have suggested that images of things to be may come into our sphere out of a being

H

where time does not exist. I have had myself no definite proof as yet that any vision
I saw was prophetic, and only one which
suggested itself as such to me, and this was
so remarkable that I put it on record, because
if it was prophetic its significance may become apparent later on. I was meditating
about twenty-one years ago in a little room,
and my meditation was suddenly broken by
a series of pictures which flashed before me
with the swiftness of moving pictures in a
theatre. They had no relation I could discover to the subject of my meditation, and
were interpolated into it then perhaps, because in a tense state of concentration when
the brain becomes luminous it is easier to
bring to consciousness what has to be brought.
I was at the time much more interested in
the politics of eternity than in the politics of
my own country, and would not have missed
an hour of my passionate meditation on the
spirit to have witnessed the most dramatic
spectacle in any of our national movements.
In this meditation I was brought to a wooded
valley beyond which was a mountain, and
between heaven and earth over the valley
was a vast figure aureoled with light, and
it descended from that circle of light and

assumed human shape, and stood before me
and looked at me. The face of this figure
was broad and noble in type, beardless and
dark-haired. It was in its breadth akin to
the face of the young Napoleon, and I would
refer both to a common archetype. This
being looked at me and vanished, and was
instantly replaced by another vision, and this
second vision was of a woman with a blue
cloak around her shoulders, who came into a
room and lifted a young child upon her lap,
and from all Ireland rays of light converged
on that child. Then this disappeared and
was on the instant followed by another
picture in the series ; and here I was brought
from Ireland to look on the coronation throne
at Westminster, and there sat on it a figure
of empire which grew weary and let fall
the sceptre from its fingers, and itself then
drooped and fell and disappeared from the
famous seat. And after that in swift succession came another scene, and a gigantic
figure, wild and distraught, beating a drum,
stalked up and down, and wherever its feet
fell there were sparks and the swirling of
flame and black smoke upward as from burn-
ing cities. It was like the Red Swineherd of
legend which beat men into an insane frenzy ;

and when that distraught figure vanished I
saw the whole of Ireland lit up from mountain
to sea, spreading its rays to the heavens as in
the vision which Brigid the seeress saw and
told to Patrick. All I could make of that
sequence was that some child of destiny,
around whom the future of Ireland was to
pivot, was born then or to be born, and that
it was to be an avatar was symbolised by the
descent of the first figure from the sky, and
that before that high destiny was to be ac-
complished the power of empire was to be
weakened, and there was to be one more
tragic episode in Irish history. Whether this
is truth or fantasy time alone can tell. No
drums that have since beaten in this land
seem to me to be mad enough to be foretold
of in that wild drumming. What can I say
of such a vision but that it impressed me
to forgetfulness of analysis, for what it said
was more important than any philosophy of
its manner. I have tried to reason over it
with myself, as I would with a sequence of
another character, to deduce from a sequence
better than could be done from a single
vision, valid reasons for believing that there
must be a conscious intellect somewhere
behind the sequence. But I cannot reason

over it. I only know that I look everywhere in the face of youth, in the aspect of
every new notability, hoping before I die to
recognise the broad-browed avatar of my
vision.

HAVE IMAGINATIONS BODY?

In the literature of science I read of marvellously delicate instruments devised to make clear to the intellect the mode of operation of forces invisible to the eye, how Alpha rays, Gamma rays, or the vibrations in metal or plant are measured, and I sigh for some device to aid the intellect in solving difficult problems of psychology. I ask myself how may I ascertain with a precision of knowledge which would convince others whether the figures of vision, imagination or dream are two or three dimensional. The figures cast on the screen in a theatre are on the flat, but have all the illusion of motion, distance, shadow, light and form. The figures of human memory I am content to accept as being in two dimensions. They are imprinted by waves of light on the retina, and cast upon some screen in the brain. But I am forced by my own experience and that of others to believe that nature has a memory, and that it is accessible to us. But this memory cannot be recorded as ours through bodily organs of sight or hearing, nor can imagination make clear to me how any medium could exist in nature which would reflect upon itself as a mirror reflects, or as human vision reflects, an impression intelligible to us of what is passing. If there were such a medium, acting as a mirror to nature or life, and retaining the impression, it must be universal as the supposed æther of the scientist; and how could impressions on this medium intelligible to us be focussed as the vibrations of light are through the needle-point of the eye to record a single view-point? In our visions of the memory of nature we see undistorted figures. If we could imagine the whole body to be sensitive to light, as is that single point in the brain on which the optic nerves converge, what kind of vision would we have? The earth under foot, objects right, left, above and below, would all clamour in various monstrous shapes for attention. The feet would see from one angle, the hands from another, back and front would confuse us; so I cannot imagine the recording power in nature as reflecting like a mirror, and retaining and recording the impressions. But we have another mode of memory in ourselves which might suggest the mode of memory in nature, that by which our subjective life is recorded. Mood, thought, passion, ecstasy, all are preserved for us, can be summoned up and re-created. How is this memory maintained ? Are we continuously casting off by way of emanation an image of ourselves instant by instant, infinitesimally delicate but yet complete ? Is every motion of mind and body preserved so that a complete facsimile, an effigy in three dimensions, exists of every moment in our being. Is the memory of nature like that ? Is it by a continuous emanation of itself it preserves for itself its own history ? Does this hypothesis lay too heavy a burden on the substance of the universe as we know it ? I do not like to use arguments the validity of which I am not myself able to establish. But I might recall that an eminent thinker in science, Balfour Stewart, supposed of the æther that there was a continual transference of energy to it from the visible universe, and that this stored-up energy might form the basis of an immortal memory for man and nature.

The conception did not lay too heavy a burden on matter as he imagined it. But what is matter? Is it not pregnant every atom of it with the infinite? Even in visible nature does not every minutest point of space reflect as a microcosm the macrocosm of earth and heaven? This minute point of space occupied by my eye as I stand on the mountain has poured into it endless vistas of manifolded mountains, vales, woods, cities, glittering seas, clouds and an infinite blueness. Wherever I move, whether by rays or waves of light, from the farthest star to the nearest leaf with its complexity of vein and tint, there comes to that pin-point of space, the eye, a multitudinous vision. If every pin-point of external space is dense yet not blind with immensity, what more miracle of subtlety, of ethereal delicacy, could be affirmed of matter and be denied because it strains belief? In that acorn which lies at my feet there is a tiny cell which has in it a memory of the oak from the beginning of earth, and a power coiled in it which can beget from itself the full majestic being of the oak. From that tiny fountain by some miracle can spring another cell, and cell after cell will be born, will go on dividing, begetting, building up from each other unnumbered myriads of cells, all controlled by some mysterious power latent in the first, so that in an hundred years they will, obeying the plan of the tiny architect, have built up "the green-robed senators of mighty woods." There is nothing incredible in the assumption that every cell in the body is wrapped about with myriad memories. He who attributes least mystery to matter is furthest from truth, and he nighest who conjectures the Absolute to be present in fullness of being in the atom. If I am reproached for the supposition that the soul of earth preserves memory of itself by casting off instant by instant enduring images of its multitudinous life, I am only saying of nature in its fullness what visible nature is doing in its own fashion without cessation. What problem of mind, vision, imagination or dream do I solve by this hypothesis? I have been perplexed as an artist by the obedience of the figures of imagination to suggestion from myself. Let me illustrate my perplexity. I imagine a group of white-robed Arabs standing on a sandy hillock and they seem of such a noble dignity that I desire

to paint them. With a restlessness akin
to that which makes a portrait - painter
arrange and rearrange his sitter, until he
gets the pose which satisfies him, I say to
myself, "I wish they would raise their arms
above their heads," and at the suggestion
all the figures in my vision raise their hands
as if in salutation of the dawn. I see other
figures in imagination which attract me as
compositions. There may be a figure sitting
down and I think it would compose better
if it was turned in another direction, and
that figure will obey my suggestion, not
always, but at times it will ; and again and
again when I who paint almost entirely from
what is called imagination, and who never
use models, watch a figure in my vision it
will change its motions as I will it. Now
this is to me amazing. The invention and
actual drawing of the intricate pattern of
light and shade involved by the lifting of
the hands of my imaginary Arabs would be
considerable. My brain does not by any
swift action foresee in detail the pictorial
consequences involved by the lifting of arms,
but yet by a single wish, a simple mental
suggestion, the intricate changes are made
in the figures of imagination as they would

be if real Arabs stood before me and raised their hands at my call. If I ask a crowd of people to whom I speak to change their position so that they may the better hear me I am not astonished at the infinite complexity of the change I bring about, because I realise that the will in each one has mastery over the form by some miracle, and the message runs along nerve and muscle, and the simple wish brings about the complex change. But how do I lay hold of the figures in dream or imagination ? By what miracle does the simple wish bring about the complex changes ? It may now be seen why I asked for some means by which I might ascertain whether the forms in dream or imagination are two or three dimensional. If they are on the flat, if they are human memories merely, vibrations of stored-up sunlight fixed in some way in the brain as a photograph is fixed, the alteration of these by a simple wish involves incredibilities. I find Freud, referring to a dream he had, saying carelessly that it was made up by a combination of memories, but yet the architecture of the dream seemed to be coherent and not a patchwork. It had motion of its own. Wonderful, indeed, that the wonder of what was written about so easily was not seen! How could we imagine even the mightiest conscious artistic intelligence, with seership into all the memories of a life, taking the vibrations which constituted this hand, and adjusting them to the vibrations which made that other arm, or even taking the vibrations which registered a complete figure and amending these so that the figure moved with different gestures from the first gestures recorded as memory? If such a picture was made up even from life-size images it would be a patchwork and the patches would show everywhere. But the dream figure or the figure of imagination will walk about with authentic motions and undistorted anatomies. Does not the effort to imagine such recombinations even by the mightiest conscious intellect involve incredibilities? At least it is so with the artist who watches form with a critical eye. How much greater the incredibility if we suppose there was no conscious artist, but that all this authentic imagery of imagination or dream came together without an intelligence to guide it? But how do we better matters if we assume that the figures in dream or imagination are three dimensional, and that they have actual

body and organisation however ethereal,
delicate or subtle ? If they are shadows
or effigies emanated from living organisms,
and are complete in their phantasmal nature
within and without it is possible to imagine
life laying hold of them. It is conceivable
that the will may direct their motions even
as at a word of command soldiers will turn
and march. That is why I suggest that the
memory of nature may be by way of emanation or shadow of life and form, and why
when we see such images they are not the
monstrous complexities they would be if
they were reflections on some universal
æther spread everywhere taking colour from
everything at every possible angle and
remaining two dimensional. The hypothesis
that everything in nature, every living
being, is a continuous fountain of phantasmal
effigies of itself would explain the way in
which ruins build up their antique life to
the eye of the seer, so that he sees the
people of a thousand years ago in their
cities which are now desolate, and the dark-
skinned merchants unrolling their bales in
the market, and this is why they appear as
some one has said, " thinking the thought and
performing the deed." If we have access to

such memories, and if they have organism within as well as without, can we not imagine will or desire of ours constraining them? Can we not imagine such forms swept into the vortex of a dreaming soul swayed by the sea of passion in which they exist and acting according to suggestion? And if we suppose that a deeper being of ours has wider vision than the waking consciousness, and can use the memories, not only of this plane of being, but of the forms peculiar to mid-world and heaven-world, this might help to solve some of the perplexities aroused in those who are intent and vigilant observers of their own dreams and imaginations. Continually in my analysis of the figures I see I am forced to follow them beyond the transitory life I know and to speculate upon the being of the Ever Living. I think there is no half-way house between the spiritual and the material where the intellect can dwell; and if we find we have our being in a universal life we must alter our values, change all our ideas until they depend upon and are in harmony with that sole cause of all that is.

INTUITION

THAT sense of a divinity ever present in
act or thought my words do not communi-
cate. The ecstatic, half-articulate, with
broken words, can make us feel the kingdom
of heaven is within him. I choose words
with reverence but speak from recollection,
and one day does not utter to another its
own wisdom. Our highest moments in life
are often those of which we hold thereafter
the vaguest memories. We may have a
momentary illumination yet retain almost as
little of its reality as ocean keeps the track
of a great vessel which went over its waters.
I remember incidents rather than moods,
vision more than ecstasy. How can I now,
passed away from myself and long at other
labours, speak of what I felt in those years
when thought was turned to the spirit, and
no duty had as yet constrained me to equal
outward effort? I came to feel akin to

those ancestors of the Aryan in remote
spiritual dawns when Earth first extended
its consciousness into humanity. In that
primal ecstasy and golden age was born that
grand spiritual tradition which still remains
embodied in Veda and Upanishad, in Persian
and Egyptian myth, and which trails glimmering with colour and romance over our own
Celtic legends. I had but a faint glow of that
which to the ancestors was full light. I
could not enter that Radiance they entered
yet Earth seemed to me bathed in an aether
of Deity. I felt at times as one raised from
the dead, made virginal and pure, who
renews exquisite intimacies with the divine
companions, with Earth, Water, Air and
Fire. To breathe was to inhale magical
elixirs. To touch Earth was to feel the
influx of power as with one who had touched
the mantle of the Lord. Thought, from
whatever it set out, for ever led to the
heavenly city. But these feelings are in-
communicable. We have no words to express a thousand distinctions clear to the
spiritual sense. If I tell of my exaltation
to another, who has not felt this himself,
it is explicable to that person as the joy
in perfect health, and he translates into

I

lower terms what is the speech of the gods
to men.

I began writing desirous to picture things
definitely to the intellect and to speak only
of that over which there could be reason and
argument, but I have often been indefinite as
when I said in an earlier chapter that earth
seemed an utterance of gods, "Every flower
was a thought. The trees were speech. The
grass was speech. The winds were speech.
The waters were speech." But what does
that convey? Many feel ecstasy at the sight
of beautiful natural objects, and it might be
said it does not interpret emotion precisely to
make a facile reference to a divine world. I
believe of nature that it is a manifestation of
Deity, and that, because we are partakers in
the divine nature, all we see has affinity with
us ; and though now we are as children who
look upon letters before they have learned to
read, to the illuminated spirit its own being
is clearly manifested in the universe even as
I recognise my thought in the words I write.
Everything in nature has intellectual significance, and relation as utterance to the Thought
out of which the universe was born, and we,
whose minds were made in its image, who
are the microcosm of the macrocosm, have in

ourselves the key to unlock the meaning of
that utterance. Because of these affinities
the spirit swiftly by intuition can interpret
nature to itself even as our humanity instinctively comprehends the character betrayed
by the curve of lips or the mood which lurks
within haunting eyes. We react in numberless ways to that myriad nature about us and
within us, but we retain for ourselves the
secret of our response, and for lack of words
speak to others of these things only in gener-
alities. I desire to be precise, and having
searched memory for some instance of that
divine speech made intelligible to myself
which I could translate into words which
might make it intelligible to others, I re-
collected something which may at least be
understood if not accepted. It was the
alphabet of the language of the gods.

This was a definite exercise of intuition
undertaken in order to evolve intellectual
order out of a chaos of impressions and to
discover the innate affinities of sound with
idea, element, force, colour and form. I
found as the inner being developed it used a
symbolism of its own. Sounds, forms and
colours, which had an established significance
in the complicated artifice of our external

intercourse with each other, took on new meanings in the spirit as if it spoke a language of its own and wished to impart it to the infant Psyche. If these new meanings did not gradually reveal an intellectual character, to pursue this meditation, to encourage the association of new ideas with old symbols would be to encourage madness. Indeed the partial uprising of such ideas, the fact that a person associates a vowel with a certain colour or a colour with a definite emotion is regarded by some as indicating incomplete sanity. I tried to light the candle on my forehead to peer into every darkness in the belief that the external universe of nature had no more exquisite architecture than the internal universe of being, and that the light could only reveal some lordlier chambers of the soul, and whatever speech the inhabitant used must be fitting for its own sphere, so I became a pupil of the spirit and tried as a child to learn the alphabet at the knees of the gods.

I was led first to brood upon the elements of human speech by that whisper of the word "Aeon" out of the darkness, for among the many thoughts I had at the time came the thought that speech may originally have been

intuitive. I discarded the idea with regard
to that word, but the general speculation
remained with me, and I recurred to it again
and again, and began brooding upon the
significance of separate letters, and had related
many letters to abstractions or elements, when
once again, seemingly by chance, I took down
a book from a shelf. It was a volume of
the Upanishads, and it opened at a page
where my eye caught this : " From that Self
came the air, from air fire, from fire water,
from water earth." I quote from a distant
memory but the words are, I think, close
enough. What excited me was that I had
already discovered what I thought were the
sound equivalents for the self, motion, fire,
water and earth ; and the order of the cosmic
evolution of the elements suggested in the
passage quoted led me to consider whether
there was any intellectual sequence in the
human sound equivalents of elements and
ideas. I then began to rearrange the roots
of speech in their natural order from throat
sounds, through dental to labials, from A
which begins to be recognisable in the throat
to M in the utterance of which the lips
are closed. An intellectual sequence of ideas
became apparent. This encouraged me to

try and complete the correspondences arrived at intuitively. I was never able to do this. Several sounds failed, however I brooded upon them, to suggest their intellectual affinities, and I can only detail my partial discoveries and indicate where harmonies may be found between my own intuitions about language and the roots of speech and in what primitive literature are intuitions akin to my own.

In trying to arrive at the affinities of sound with thought I took letter after letter, brooding upon them, murmuring them again and again, and watching intensely every sensation in consciousness, every colour, form or idea which seemed evoked by the utterance. No doubt the sanity of the boy who walked about the roads at night more than thirty years ago murmuring letters to himself with the reverence of a mystic murmuring the Ineffable Name might have been questioned by any one who knew that he was trying to put himself in the place of his Aryan ancestors, and to find as they might have found the original names for earth, air, water, fire, the forces and elements of the nature which was all about them. Even as in the myth in Genesis beings were named by the earliest man, so I invited the Heavenly Man to renew for me that first speech, and to name the elements as they were by those who looked up at the sky, and cried out the name of the fire in the sky from a God-given intuition.

THE LANGUAGE OF THE GODS

If I interpreted rightly that dweller in the mind, the true roots of human speech are vowels and consonants, each with affinity to idea, force, colour and form, the veriest abstractions of these, but by their union into words expressing more complex notions, as atoms and molecules by their union form the compounds of the chemist. It is difficult to discover single words of abstract significance to represent adequately the ideas associated with these rudiments of speech. Every root is charged with significance, being the symbol of a force which is itself the fountain of many energies, even as primordial being when manifested rolls itself out into numberless forms, states of energy and consciousness. The roots of human speech are the sound correspondences of powers which in their combination and interaction make up the universe. The mind of man is made in the image of Deity, and the elements of speech are related to the powers in his mind and through it to the being of the Oversoul.

These true roots of language are few, alphabet and roots being identical. The first root is A, the sound symbol for the self in man and Deity in the cosmos. Its form equivalent is the circle ◯. The second root is R, representing motion. Its colour correspondence is red, and its form symbol is the line |.

Motion engenders heat, and the third root following the order from throat sounds to labials is H, the sound correspondence of Heat. Its symbol is the triangle Δ, and it has affinity with the colour orange.

Motion and heat are the begetters of Fire, the sound equivalent of which is the root L, which in form is symbolised by lines radiating from a point as in this figure 人. L is fire, light or radiation, and it is followed in the series of roots by Y which symbolises the reaction in nature against that radiation of energy. It is the sound equivalent of binding, concentration or condensation. Matter in the cosmos is obeying the law of gravitation and gathering into fire-mists preliminary to its knotting into suns and planets. The colour affinity is yellow. In man it is will which focuses energy and concentrates it to a burning-point for the accomplishing of desire. Its form symbol is ༉ representing a vortex or spiral movement inward, opposing in this the expansion or radiation implied in the root L.

The root which follows Y is W, the sound symbol of liquidity or water. Its form is semilunar, ᴗ, and I think its colour is green.

We have now descended to earth and with this descent comes dualism, and henceforth all the roots have companion roots. Primordial substance has lost its ethereal character and has settled into a solid or static condition. The two roots which express this are G and K ; G is the symbol of earth, as K is of mineral, rock, crystal or hardness of any kind. I could discover with no certainty any colour affinities for either of these roots, and about the forms I am also uncertain though I was moved to relate G with the square ☐ and K with the square crossed by a diagonal ◈.

The twin roots next in the series are S and Z, and I can find no better words to indicate the significance of the first than impregnation, inbreathing or insouling. We have reached in evolution the stage when the one life breaks into myriads of lives, which on earth finds its correspondence in the genesis of the cell. Z represents the multiplication, division or begetting of organism from organism. It is the outbreathing or bringing to birth of the seed which is sown. The form symbol of S is, I think, O, and of Z ⊕. I discovered no colour affinities for either.

The duality of roots succeeding this is TH and SH. The first is the sound equivalent of growth, expansion or swelling, and its twin root represents that state where the limit of growth in a particular form is reached and a scattering or dissolution of its elements takes place. In the vegetable world we might find an illustration in the growth and decay of a plant.

After these twain come the duality of T and D. I found great difficulty in discovering words to express the abstractions related to these. Yet in meditating on them with reference to the T, I was continually haunted by the idea of individual action, movement or initiative, and I believe it refers to that state when life divorced from its old interior

unity with the source of life, and, confined in
a form, begins in its imagination of itself to
be an ego, is in a state of outgoing, acts and
looks outward, touches and tastes ; while D
represents the reverse side of that, its reaction or absorption inward to silence, sleep,
immobility, abeyance. The form symbol
T is + and ⌂ vaguely suggested itself to
me as the symbol of D.

There is a parallelism between T and TH
as there is between D and SH, T representing movement of the thing by itself while
TH represents growth or expansion merely,
while D represents the more subjective
sinking of a thing into abeyance of its
powers as SH represents the external resolv-
ing of an organism into its elements.

For the dualism of roots J and TCH my
intuition failed utterly to discover correla-
tions, and when I had placed the roots in
their correct sequence and endeavoured by
intellect and reason to arrive at the logical
significance these two might have in the
series of sounds, I could never satisfy myself
that I had come nigh to any true affinity,
so I pass these by.

The roots which follow are V and F, of
which the first refers to life in water, to all

that swims, while F is related to what lives in air and flies. I am doubtful about the form symbols, but colour affinities began here again, and blue suggested itself to me as the correspondence, while the twin roots which come after them, P and B, are related to indigo, the dark blue.

Life has now reached the human stage, is divided into sexes, and P is the sound symbol for life masculine or paternity, while B represents feminine life or maternity.

The series closes with N and M. The first of these represents continuance of being, immortality if you will, while the last root, in the utterance of which the lips are closed, has the sense of finality, it is the close, limit, measure, end or death of things. Their colour affinities are with violet. In all there are twenty-one consonants which with the vowels make up the divine roots of speech.

The vowels are the sound symbols of consciousness in seven moods or states, while the consonants represent states of matter and modes of energy.

I despair of any attempt to differentiate from each other the seven states of consciousness represented by the vowels. How shall I make clear the difference between A where consciousness in man or cosmos begins manifestation, utterance or limitation of itself, and OO where consciousness is returning into itself, breaking from the limitation of form and becoming limitless once more ; or E when it has become passional, or I where it has become egoistic, actively intellectual or reasoning, or O where it has become intuitional. Our psychology gives me no names for these states, but the vowel root always represents consciousness, and, in its union with the consonant root, modifies or defines its significance, doing that again as it precedes or follows it. I once held more completely than I do now an interior apprehension of the significance of all, and I might perhaps, if I had concentrated more intently, have completed more fully the correspondences with idea, colour and form. But life attracts us in too many ways, and when I was young and most sensitive and intuitional I did not realise the importance of what I was attempting to do.

This so far as I know is the only considered effort made by any one to ascertain the value of intuition as a faculty by using it in reference to matters where the intellect was useless but where the results attained by intuition could be judged by the reason. Intuition is a faculty of which many speak with veneration, but it seems rarely to be evoked consciously, and, if it is witness to a knower in man, it surely needs testing and use like any other faculty. I have exercised intuition with respect to many other matters and with inward conviction of the certainty of truth arrived at in this way, but they were matters relating to consciousness and were not by their nature easily subject to ratification by the reason. These intuitions in respect of language are to some extent capable of being reasoned or argued over, and I submit them for consideration by others whose study of the literature, learning and language of the ancients may give them special authority.

ANCIENT INTUITIONS

Even where I had a certitude that my attribution of element, form or colour to a root was right I have never thought this exhausted the range of its affinities in our manifold being. I went but a little way within myself, but felt that greater powers awaited discovery within us, powers whose shadowy skirts flicker on the surface of consciousness but with motion so impalpable that we leave them nameless. The root I relate to light may have correspondence also with another power which is to the dark divinity of being what light is to the visible world. I have never thought that the languages spoken by men had all their origin in one intuitional speech. There may have been many beginnings in that undiscoverable antiquity. But I believe that one, or perhaps several, among the early races, more spiritual than the rest, was prompted by intuition, while others may have developed speech in any of the ways suggested by biologists and scholars. The genius of some races leads them to seek for light within as the genius of others leads them to go outward. I imagine a group of the ancestors lit up from within, endowed with the primal blessings of youth and ecstasy, the strings of their being not frayed as ours are, nor their God-endowed faculties abused, still exquisitely sensitive, feeling those kinships and affinities with the elements which are revealed in the sacred literature of the Aryan, and naming these affinities from an impulse springing up within. I can imagine the spirit struggling outwards making of element, colour, form or sound a mirror, on which, outside itself, it would find symbols of all that was pent within itself, and so gradually becoming self-conscious in the material nature in which it was embodied, but which was still effigy or shadow of a divine original. I can imagine them looking up at the fire in the sky, and calling out " El " if it was the light they adored, or if they rejoiced in the heat and light together they would name it " Hel." Or if they saw death, and felt it as the stillness or ending of motion

K

or breath, they would say "Mor." Or if
the fire acting on the water made it boil,
they would instinctively combine the sound
equivalents of water and fire, and "Wal"
would be the symbol. If the fire of life was
kindled in the body to generate its kind, the
sound symbol would be "Lub." When the
axe was used to cut, its hardness would
prompt the use of the hard or metallic affinity
in sound, and "Ak" would be to cut or
pierce. One extension of meaning after
another would rapidly increase the wealth of
significance, and recombinations of roots the
power of expression. The root "M" with
its sense of finality would suggest "Mi" to
diminish, and as to measure a thing is to go
to its ends, "Ma" would also mean to measure,
and as to think a thing is to measure it,
"Ma" would also come to be associated
with thinking. I had nearly all my correspondences vividly in mind before I inquired
of friends more learned than myself what
were the reputed origins of human speech,
and in what books I could find whatever
knowledge there was, and then I came upon
the Aryan roots ; and there I thought and
still think are to be found many evidences in
corroboration of my intuitions. There are

pitfalls for one who has no pretensions to scholarship in tracking words to their origins, and it is a labour for the future in conjunction with one more learned than myself to elucidate these intuitions in regard to the roots, and to go more fully into the psychology which led to rapid extension of meanings until words were created, which at first sight seem to have no relation to the root values. I still believe I can see in the Aryan roots an intelligence struggling outward from itself to recognise its own affinities in sound. But I wish here only to give indications and directions of approach to that Divine Mind whose signature is upon us in everything, and whose whole majesty is present in the least thing in nature. I have written enough to enable those who are curious to exercise their intuitions or analytic faculty in conjunction with their scholarship, to test the worth of my intuitions. Intuition must be used in these correspondences, for the art of using them is not altogether discoverable by the intellect. I hope also that my partial illumination will be completed, corrected or verified by others.

A second line of investigation I suggest is the study of some harmony of primitive alphabets, such as that compiled by Forster, and, after arranging the letters in their natural order from throat sounds to labials, to see if there is not much to lead us to suppose that there was an original alphabet, where the form equivalents of sound proceeded in an orderly way from the circle through the line, the triangle and the other forms I have indicated. Perhaps the true correspondences were retained as an esoteric secret by the wisest, because there may have been in them the key to mysteries only to be entrusted to those many times tested before the secret of the use of power was disclosed. And again I would suggest a study of that science of divine correspondences which is embodied in mystical Indian literature. The correspondences of form, colour or force with letters given there are not always in agreement with my own. Sometimes as in the Bagavadgita where Krishna, the Self of the Manifested Universe, says, " I am the A among letters," I find agreement. In other works like the Shivagama there is partial agreement as where it says, " Meditate upon the fire force with R as its symbol, as being triangular and red." The colour and the letter are here in harmony with my own intuitions, but the form is not, and I am more inclined to believe my own intuition to be true because I find in so many of the primitive alphabets the form symbol of R is the line coming out of a circle. The water force is given in the same book a semilunar form as correspondence, but its sound symbol is given as V and not W. The earth force is given as quadrangular in form as I imagine it, but the colour is yellow. I have not investigated the consonants in their attribution to the nervous system given in such books. I have no doubt that in a remoter antiquity the roots of language were regarded as sacred, and when chanted every letter was supposed to stir into motion or evoke some subtle force in the body. Tone and word combined we know will thrill the nervous system, and this is specially so with lovers of music and persons whose virgin sensitiveness of feeling has never been blunted by excess. A word chanted or sung will start the wild fires leaping in the body, like hounds which hear their master calling them by name, and to those whose aspiration heavenward has purified their being there comes at last a moment when at the calling of the Ineffable Name the Holy Breath rises as a flame and the shadow man goes forth to become one with the ancestral self.

What is obvious in that ancient literature is the belief in a complete circle of correspondences between every root sound in the human voice and elements, forms and colours, and that the alphabet was sacred in character. Intuitions which modern psychologists regard as evidence of decadence are found present in the literature of antiquity. The attributions sometimes are the same as mine ; sometimes they differ, but they suggest the same theory of a harmony of microcosm with macrocosm, and it is carried out so that every centre in the body is named by the name of a divine power. It is only by a spiritual science we can recover identity, renew and make conscious these affinities. Life had other labours for me from which I could not escape, and I had not for long the leisure in which to reknit the ties between myself and the ancestral being. But while I still had leisure I experienced those meltings of the external into intelligible meanings. The form of a flower long brooded upon would translate itself into energies, and these would resolve themselves finally into states of consciousness, intelligible to me while I experienced them, but too

remote from the normal for words to tell
their story.   I may have strayed for a moment
into that Garden of the Divine Mind where,
as it is said in Genesis, "He made every
flower before it was in the field and every
herb before it grew."   My failure to find
words to express what I experienced made
me concentrate more intensely upon the
relation of form and colour to consciousness
in the hope that analysis might make intellectual exposition possible.   I do not wish
to linger too long on the analysis I made.
The message of nature is more important than
the symbols used to convey it, and, in de-
tailing these correspondences, I feel rather as
one who reading Shelley's "Hymn of Pan"
ignored all that ecstasy and spoke merely of
spelling or verse structure.   But why do I
say that ?   The works of the Magician of the
Beautiful are not like ours and in the least
fragment His artistry is no less present than
in the stars.   We may enter the infinite
through the minute no less than through
contemplation of the vast.   I thought in that
early ecstasy of mine when I found how near
to us was the King in His Beauty that I could
learn to read that marvellous writing on the
screen of Nature and teach it to others ; and,

as a child first learns its letters with difficulty, but after a time leaps to the understanding of their combination, and later, without care for letters or words, follows out the thought alone ; so I thought the letters of the divine utterance might be taught and the spirit in man would leap by intuition to the thought of the Spirit making that utterance. For all that vast ambition I have not even a complete alphabet to show, much less one single illustration of how to read the letters of nature in their myriad intricacies of form, colour and sound in the world we live in. But I believe that vision has been attained by the seers, and we shall all at some time attain it, and, as is said in the Divine Shepherd of Hermes, it shall meet us everywhere, plain and easy, walking or resting, waking or sleeping, "for there is nothing which is not the image of God."

POWER

I HAVE spoken of a training of the will, but have not indicated the spring of power in our being, nor dilated on those moments when we feel a Titanic energy lurks within us ready to our summons as the familiar spirit to the call of the enchanter. If we have not power we are nothing and must remain outcasts of the Heavens. We must be perfect as the Father is perfect. If in the being of the Ancient of Days there is power, as there is wisdom and beauty, we must liken ourselves to that being, partake, as our nature will permit, of its power, or we can never enter it. The Kingdom is taken by violence. The easier life becomes in our civilisations, the remoter we are from nature, the more does power ebb away from most of us. It ebbs away for all but those who never relax the will but sustain it hour by hour. We even grow to dread the powerful person because we feel how phantasmal before power are beauty and wisdom, and indeed there is no true beauty or wisdom which is not allied with strength. For one who cultivates will in himself there are thousands who cultivate the intellect or follow after beauty, and that is because the intellect can walk easily on the level places, while at first every exercise of the will is laborious as the lift is to the climber of a precipice. Few are those who come to that fullness of power where the will becomes a fountain within them perpetually springing up self-fed, and who feel like the mountain lovers who know that it is easier to tread on the hilltops than to walk on the low and level roads. Because in our ordered life power is continually ebbing away from us, nature, which abhors a vacuum in our being, is perpetually breaking up our civilisations by wars or internal conflicts, so that stripped of our ease, in battle, through struggle and sacrifice, we may grow into power again ; and this must continue until we tread the royal road, and cultivate power in our being as we cultivate beauty or intellect. Those who have in themselves the highest power, who are miracle-workers, the Buddhas and the Christs, are also the teachers of peace,

and they may well be so having themselves
attained mastery of the Fire.

It is because it is so laborious to cultivate
the will we find in literature endless analysis
of passion and thought, but rarely do we
find one writing as if he felt the powers
leaping up in his body as the thronged
thoughts leap up in the brain. I was never
able to recognise that harmony of powers
spoken of by the ancients as inhabiting the
house of the body, lurking in nerve-centre
or plexus, or distinguish their functions, but
I began to feel, after long efforts at concentration and mastery of the will, the beginning of an awakening of the fires, and at
times there came partial perception of the
relation of these forces to centres in the
psychic body. I could feel them in myself;
and sometimes see them, or the vibration or
light of them, about others who were seekers
with myself for this knowledge; so that the
body of a powerful person would appear to
be throwing out light in radiation from head
or heart, or plumes of fire would rise above
the head jetting from fountains within,
apparitions like wings of fire, plumes or
feathers of flame, or dragon-like crests, many-
coloured. Once at the apex of intensest

meditation I awoke that fire in myself of which the ancients have written, and it ran up like lightning along the spinal cord, and my body rocked with the power of it, and I seemed to myself to be standing in a fountain of flame, and there were fiery pulsations as of wings about my head, and a musical sound not unlike the clashing of cymbals with every pulsation ; and if I had remembered the ancient wisdom I might have opened that eye which searches infinitude. But I remembered only, in a half terror of the power I had awakened, the danger of misdirection of the energy, for such was the sensation of power that I seemed to myself to have opened the seal of a cosmic fountain, so I remained contemplative and was not the resolute guider of the fire. And indeed this rousing of the fire is full of peril ; and woe to him who awakens it before he has purified his being into selflessness, for it will turn downward and vitalise his darker passions and awaken strange frenzies and inextinguishable desires. The turning earthward of that heaven-born power is the sin against the Holy Breath, for that fire which leaps upon us in the ecstasy of contemplation of Deity is the Holy Breath, the power which can

carry us from Earth to Heaven. It is
normally known to man only in procreation,
but its higher and mightier uses are unknown
to him. Even though in our scriptures it
is said of it that it gives to this man vision
or the discerning of spirits, and to that
poetry or eloquence, and to another healing
and magical powers, it remains for most a
myth of the theologians, and is not mentioned
by any of our psychologists though it is the
fountain out of which is born all other
powers in the body and is the sustainer of
all our faculties. Normally I found this
power in myself, not leaping up Titanically
as if it would storm the heavens, but a steady
light in the brain, "the candle upon the
forehead," and it was revealed in ecstasy of
thought or power in speech, and in a continuous welling up from within myself of
intellectual energy, vision or imagination.
It is the afflatus of the poet or musician.
As an ancient scripture says of it, "The
Illuminator is the inspirer of the poet, the
jeweller, the chiseller and all who work in
the arts." It is the Promethean fire, and
only by mastery of this power will man be
able to ascend to the ancestral Paradise.
Again and again I would warn all who read

of the danger of awakening it, and again and again I would say that without this power we are as nothing.   We shall never scale the Heavens, and religions, be they ever so holy, will never open the gates to us, unless we are able mightily to open them for ourselves and enter as the strong spirit who cannot be denied.   This power might cry of itself to us :

My kinsmen are they, beauty, wisdom, love ;
But without me are none may dare to climb
To the Ancestral Light that glows above
    Its mirrored lights in Time.

King have I been and foe in ages past.
None may escape me.   I am foe until
There shall be for the spirit forged at last
    The high unshakable will.

Fear, I will rend you.   Love, I make you strong.
Wed with my might the beautiful and wise.
We shall go forth at last, a Titan throng,
    To storm His Paradise.

THE MEMORY OF THE SPIRIT

Hy Brazil, Ildathach, the lands of Immortal Youth which flush with magic the dreams of childhood, for most sink soon below far horizons and do not again arise. For around childhood gather the wizards of the darkness and they baptize it and change its imagination of itself as in the Arabian tales of enchantment men were changed by sorcerers who cried, " Be thou beast or bird." So by the black art of education is the imagination of life about itself changed, and one will think he is a worm in the sight of Heaven, he who is but a god in exile, and another of the Children of the King will believe that he is the offspring of animals. What palaces they were born in, what dominions they are rightly heir to, are concealed from them as in the fairy tale the stolen prince lives obscurely among the swineherds. Yet at times men do not remember, in dream and in the deeps of sleep, they still wear sceptre and diadem and partake of the banquet of the gods. The gods are still living. They are our brothers. They await us. They beckon us to come up to them and sit upon equal thrones. To those who cry out against romance I would say, You yourself are romance. You are the lost prince herding obscurely among the swine. The romance of your spirit is the most marvellous of stories. Your wanderings have been greater than those of Ulysses. You have been Bird of Paradise and free of immensity, and you have been outcast and wingless, huddled under the rocks and despairing of the Heavens. If you will but awaken the inner sight, Hy Brazil, Ildathach, all the lands of Immortal Youth will build themselves up anew for you no longer as fantasy but in vivid actuality. Earth will become magical and sweet as ever. You will be drunken with beauty. You may see the fiery eyes of the Cyclops wandering over the mountains and hear the Bell Branch shaken, the sound that summons the spirit home. From long pondering I have come to believe in the eternity of the spirit and that it is an inhabitant of many spheres, for

I know not how otherwise I can interpret to myself the myriad images that as memories or imaginations cling to it, following it into the body as birds follow the leader in the migratory flock. Looking back on that other life which began to dominate this there are a thousand things I cannot understand except I believe that for myself and for all of us there has been an eternity of being and that many spheres are open to us. If these images are not earth-born, from what land, Elfland, Heaven-world or God-world, do they come ? I have chosen but a few images out of many to explain why I think our dreams and visions come often in all completeness into our sphere out of other spheres of being and are not built up from memories of earth. Looking back upon that other life through the vistas of memory I see breaking in upon the images of this world forms of I know not what antiquity. I walk out of strange cities steeped in the jewel glow and gloom of evening, or sail in galleys over the silvery waves of the antique ocean. I reside in tents, or in palace chambers, go abroad in chariots, meditate in cyclopean buildings, am worshipper of the Earth gods upon the mountains, lie tranced in Egyptian

L

crypts, or brush with naked body through the long sunlit grasses of the prairies. Endlessly the procession of varying forms goes back into remote yesterdays of the world. How do these self-conceptions spring up? How are they clothed with the state of ancient civilisations? If when I perceived them they were the newest things in the world, and the images were minted that instant by the imagination, out of what treasury of design came the fitting scenery, the always varied buildings, garments and setting of wood, plain or mountain? Are they not rather, I ask myself, memories of the spirit incarnated many times? And if so, again I ask myself is it only on earth there has been this long ancestry of self? For there is another self in me which seemed to know not the world but revealed itself to the listening bodily life in cosmic myths, in remote legends of the Children of Darkness and the Children of Light, and of the revolt against heaven. And another self seemed to bring with it vision or memory of elemental beings, the shining creatures of water and wood, or who break out in opalescent colour from the rocks or hold their court beneath the ponderous hills. And there was another self which was akin to the gloomy world of the shades, but recoiled shuddering from them. And there was yet another self which sought out after wisdom, and all these other selves and their wisdom and memories were but tributary to it. The gates of sleep too were often thronged with fleeting presences as I sank into unconsciousness, or was outcast from that innermost being when waking, and I saw but for an instant back into the profundity, and at times it appeared to the imagination as the gate of Eden :

With dreadful faces thronged and fiery arms.

Out of what sphere came that being taller and mightier than human, whose body seemed wrought out of flame and whose eyes had the stillness of an immortal, and who seemed to gaze at me out of eternity as I waked in the night. It was so lofty and above humanity that I seemed to myself to be less than an insect, though something in me cried out to it in brotherhood, and I knew not whether I had fallen from its height, or was a lost comrade lagging far behind in time who should have been equal and companion but was too feeble to rise to such majesty. I know that I have not been alone in such imaginations for there are few whose intent will has tried to scale the Heavens who have not been met by messages from the gods who are the fountains of this shadowy beauty, and who are, I think, ourselves beyond this mirage of time and space by which we are enchanted.   I have spoken to others, seekers like myself upon this quest, and recognise identity of vision and experience.   But I have not been able to devote to every mental image the thought which might make its meaning or origin intelligible.   We cannot do that for the forms we see move continuously in visible nature, for we pass them by thinking intensely but of a few of them.   But our psychology must take account of every experience of the soul.   I have not found in latter-day philosophical writers the explanation of my own experiences, and I think that is because there has been an over-development of intellect and few have cultivated vision, and without that we have not got the first data for fruitful speculation.   We rarely find philosophical writers referring to vision of their own, yet we take them as guides on our mental travelling, though in this world we all would prefer to have knowledge of earth and heaven through the eyes of a child rather than to know them only through the musings of one who was blind, even though his intellect was mighty as Kant's.

It is only when I turn to the literature of vision and intuition, to the sacred books and to half sacred tradition, to the poets and seers, that I find a grandiose conception of nature in which every spiritual experience is provided for. I have not entered the paradises they entered but what little I know finds its place in the universe of their vision. Whether they are Syrian, Greek, Egyptian or Hindu, the writers of the sacred books seem to me as men who had all gazed upon the same august vision and reported of the same divinity. Even in our own Gaelic wonder tales I often find a vision which is, I think, authentic, and we can, I believe, learn from these voyages to the Heaven-world more of the geography of the spirit and the many mansions in the being of the Father than we can from the greatest of our sightless philosophers. The Earth-world, Mid-world, Heaven-world and God-world spoken of in the Indian scriptures are worlds our Gaelic ancestors had also knowledge of. When Cormac enters the Heaven-world and is told by those who inhabit it,

"Whenever we imagine the fields to be sown they are sown. Whenever we imagine the fields to be reaped they are reaped," he saw the same world as the seer who wrote in the marvellous Upanishad: "There are no chariots there or roads for chariots. The soul makes for itself chariots and roads for chariots. There are no joys or rejoicings there. The soul makes for itself joys and rejoicings. For the spirit of man is creator." The visionaries of the future will finally justify the visionaries of the past. I do not feel that my knowledge is great enough to do this, nor have I been able to steal from a life made busy by other labours enough time or enough thought even to use in the best way the little I know. I would like to vindicate my predecessors in Ireland and correlate my own vision and the vision of my friends with the vision of those who went before us, for I think when we discard the past and its vision we are like men who, half-way up a mountain, decide foolishly to attempt the ascent from another side of the hill and so continually lose the height which was gained. Our Gaelic ancestors had the gift of seership, and I had thought at one time to reconstruct from the ancient literature the vision of the universe they had, a labour which might be done by any who had vision of his own and who was versed in the comparative study of the religions of the past, and so make intelligible to those who live here to-day the thought of their forefathers, and enable them to begin anew the meditation towards divine things so often broken up in our unhappy history. All literature tends to produce a sacred book by an evolution of thought of the highest minds building one upon another. A literature so continually imaginative, visionary and beautiful as the Gaelic would, I do not doubt, have culminated in some magnificent expression of the spirit if life had not been drawn from central depths to surfaces by continuous invasions. I think that meditation is beginning anew, and the powers which were present to the ancestors are establishing again their dominion over the spirit. To some there come startling flashes of vision, and others feel a hand of power touching them thrust out from a hidden world. Whether they know it or not they are the servants of gods who speak or act through them and make them the messengers of their will. I have written down some of my own thoughts and experiences that others may be encouraged to believe that by imagination they can lay hold of truth ; and as something must be written about the geography of the spirit by way of guidance to those who rise within themselves in meditation I will try briefly to reconstruct the Celtic vision of Heaven and Earth as I believe it was known to the Druids and bardic seers.   Let no one who requires authority read what I have written for I will give none.   If the spirit of the reader does not bear witness to truth he will not be convinced even though a Whitley Stokes rose up to verify the written word. Let it be accepted by others as a romantic invention or attribution of divine powers to certain names to make more coherent the confusion of Celtic myth.

CELTIC COSMOGONY

In the beginning was the boundless Lir, an infinite depth, an invisible divinity, neither dark nor light, in whom were all things past and to be. There at the close of a divine day, time being ended, and the Nuts of Knowledge harvested, the gods partake of the Feast of Age and drink from a secret fountain. Their being there is neither life nor death nor sleep nor dream, but all are wondrously wrought together. They lie in the bosom of Lir, cradled in the same peace, those who hereafter shall meet in love or war in hate. The Great Father and the Mother of the Gods mingle together and Heaven and Earth are lost, being one in the Infinite Lir.

Of Lir but little may be affirmed, and nothing can be revealed. In trance alone the seer might divine beyond his ultimate vision this being. It is a breath with many voices which cannot speak in one tone, but utters itself through multitudes. It is beyond the gods and if they were to reveal it, it could only be through their own departure and a return to the primeval silences. But in this is the root of existence from which springs the sacred Hazel whose branches are the gods : and as the mystic night trembles into dawn, its leaves and its blossoms and its starry fruit burgeon simultaneously and are shed over the waters of space. An image of futurity has arisen in the divine imagination : and Sinan, who is also Dana, the Great Mother and Spirit of Nature, grows thirsty to receive its imprint on her bosom, and to bear again her offspring of stars and starry beings. Then the first fountain is opened and seven streams issue like seven fiery whirlwinds, and Sinan is carried away and mingled with the torrent, and when the force of the torrent is broken, Sinan also meets death.

What other names Connla's Well and the Sacred Hazel have in Celtic tradition may be discovered later, but here, without reference to names, which only bewilder until their significance is made known, it is better to explain with less of symbol this Celtic Cosmogenesis.

We have first of all Lir, an infinite being, neither spirit nor energy nor substance, but rather the spiritual form of these, in which all the divine powers, raised above themselves, exist in a mystic union or trance. This is the night of the gods from which Mananan first awakens, the most spiritual divinity known to the ancient Gael, being the Gaelic equivalent of that Spirit which breathed on the face of the waters. He is the root of existence from which springs the Sacred Hazel, the symbol of life ramifying everywhere : and the forms of this life are conceived first by Mananan, the divine imagination. It throws itself into seven forms or divinities, the branches of the Hazel ; and these again break out endlessly into leaves and blossoms and fruit, into myriads of divine beings, the archetypes and ancestral begetters of those spirits who are the Children of Lir. All these are first in the Divine Darkness and are unrevealed, and Mananan is still the unuttered Word, and is in that state the Chaldaic oracle of Proclus saith of the Divine Mind : " It had not yet gone forth, but abode in the Paternal Depth, and in the adytum of god - nourished Silence."

But Mananan, while one in essence with the Paternal Lir, is yet, as the divine imagination, a separate being to whom, thus brooding, Lir seems apart, or covered over with a veil, and this aspect of Lir, a mirage which begins to cover over true being, is Dana, the Hibernian Mother of the Gods, or Sinan in the antique Dinn-shenchus, deity first viewed externally, and therefore seeming to partake of the nature of substance, and, as the primal form of matter, the Spirit of Nature. Mananan alone of all the gods exists in the inner side of this spirit, and therefore it is called his mantle, which, flung over man or god, wraps them from the gaze of embodied beings. His mantle, the Faed Fia, has many equivalents in other mythologies. It is the Aether within which Zeus runs invisibly, and the Akasa through which Brahm sings his eternal utterance of joy. The mantle of Mananan, the Aether, the Akasa, were all associated with Sound as a creative power, for to the mystic imagination of the past the world was upsung into being ; and what other thought inspired the apostle who wrote, " In the beginning was the Word " ?

Out of the Divine Darkness Mananan
has arisen, a brooding twilight before dawn,
in which the cloud images of the gods are
thronging.   But there is still in Lir an
immense deep of being, an emotional life
too vast, too spiritual, too remote to speak
of, for the words we use to-day cannot tell
its story.   It is the love yet unbreathed,
and yet not love, but rather a hidden
unutterable tenderness, or joy, or the
potency of these, which awakens as the
image of the divine imagination is reflected
in the being of the Mother, and then it
rushes forth to embrace it.   The Fountain
beneath the Hazel has broken.   Creation
is astir.   The Many are proceeding from
the One.   An energy or love or eternal
desire has gone forth which seeks through
a myriad forms of illusion for the infinite
being it has left.   It is Angus the Young,
an eternal joy becoming love, a love changing
into desire, and leading on to earthly passion
and forgetfulness of its own divinity.   The
eternal joy becomes love when it has first
merged itself in form and images of a divine
beauty dance before it and lure it afar.
This is the first manifested world, the
Tirnanoge or World of Immortal Youth.

The love is changed into desire as it is drawn deeper into nature, and this desire builds up the Mid-world or World of the Waters. And, lastly, as it lays hold of the earthly symbol of its desire it becomes on Earth that passion which is spiritual death. In another sense Angus may be described as the passing into activity of a power latent in Lir, working through the divine imagination, impressing its ideations on nature in its spiritual state, and thereby causing its myriad transformations. It is the fountain in which every energy has its birth, from the power which lays the foundations of the world, down through love and every form of desire to chemical affinity, just as Mananan is the root of all conscious life, from the imperial being of the gods down to the consciousness in the ant or amœba. So is Dana also the basis of every material form from the imperishable body of the immortals to the transitory husk of the gnat. As this divinity emerges from its primordial state of ecstatic tenderness or joy in Lir, its divided rays, incarnate in form, enter upon a threefold life of spiritual love, of desire, and the dark shadow of love ; and these three states have for themselves three worlds into which they have transformed the primal nature of Dana : a World of Immortal Youth : a Mid-world where everything changes with desire : and which is called from its fluctuations the World of the Waters : and lastly, the Earth-world where matter has assumed that solid form when it appears inanimate or dead. The force of the fountain which whirled Sinan away has been spent and Sinan has met death.

The conception of Angus as an all-pervading divinity who first connects being with non-being seems removed by many aeons of thought from that beautiful golden-haired youth who plays on the tympan surrounded by singing birds. But the golden-haired Angus of the bards has a relation to the earlier Eros, for in the mysteries of the Druids all the gods sent bright witnesses of their boundless being, who sat enthroned in the palaces of the Sidhe, and pointed the way to the Land of Promise to the man who dared become more than man.

But what in reality is Angus and what is Dana, and how can they be made real to us ? They will not be gained by much reading of

the legendary tales, for they are already
with us. A child sits on the grass and the
sunlight falls about it. It is lulled by the
soft colour. It grows dreamy, a dreaminess
filled with a vague excitement. It feels a
pleasure, a keen magnetic joy at the touch
of earth : or it lays its head in a silent
tenderness nigh a mother or sister, its mood
impelling it to grow nearer to something it
loves. That tenderness in the big dreamy
heart of childhood is Angus, and the mother-
love it divines is Dana ; and the form which
these all-pervading divinities take in the
heart of the child and the mother, on the
one side desire, on the other a profound
tenderness or pity, are nearest of all the
moods of earth to the first Love and the
Mighty Mother, and through them the
divine may be vaguely understood. If the
desire remains pure, through innocence, or
by reason of wisdom, it becomes in the
grown being a constant preoccupation with
spiritual things, or in words I have quoted
before where it is better said, " The inexpressible yearning of the inner man to go out
into the infinite."

Of Dana, the Hibernian Mother of the
gods, I have already said she is the first

spiritual form of matter, and therefore Beauty. As every being emerges out of her womb clothed with form, she is the Mighty Mother, and as mother of all she is that divine compassion which exists beyond and is the final arbiter of the justice of the gods. Her heart will be in ours when ours forgive.

THE CELTIC IMAGINATION

OTHER names might be used in this Celtic cosmogenesis and the Dagda stand for Lir, Boan for Dana, Fintan for Mananan, and others again might be interchangeable with these. Even as the generations follow one another in time, each looking upon the same unchanging nature as the ancestors but naming it by other names, so in antiquity races were invaded by others who came with a cosmogony the same in all essentials, but for differences of language and name, as that of the people invaded. After centuries there comes a blending of cultures and a subsidence into legend, bringing about a bewildering mosaic of mythology. The unity of primeval vision is broken up in the prism of literature. Deities grow in number in the popular imagination and coexist there, who in truth, if their spiritual ancestry was known, were but varying names for one divine being.

There are several mythologies in Irish legend the figures of which are made contemporary with each other by the later poets, and while it might be of interest to scholars to disentangle these and relate each deity to its proper cycle, only the vision of the universe which underlay them all is of real importance. That spiritual Overworld our Gaelic ancestors beheld was in essentials the same as the Overworld revealed in the sacred books ; and in the wonder tales of the Gael we find a great secular corroboration of sacred literature and of half-sacred philosophy such as Plato utters through the lips of Socrates. Earth, Midworld, Heaven-world and the great deep of deity they knew as they are expounded in the Upanishads. We can discern the same vision in the Apostle whose beginning of things was in the fulness of being out of which arose the Christos or divine imagination, in which, as it went forth on its cyclic labours, life or the Holy Breath was born, or became in it, and these again shine and work in the darkness of earth. And when St. Paul speaks of a third heaven we divine he had risen to the world of the Christos and was there initiated into mysteries of which it was not lawful to speak. In the sacred books there is a profounder life than there is in secular literature where there is vision indeed, but in the sacred books there is the being. The mind in retrospect, meditation and aspiration needs guidance ; and this spiritual architecture of Earth-world, with Mid-world, Heaven-world and God-world rising above it, made my own vision so far as it went intelligible to me, for my disconnected glimpses of supernature seemed to find a place in that architecture of the heavens. In earlier pages I described my first visions of other planes, and the beings there, how some were shining and how others were a lordlier folk lit up from within as if a sun was hidden in the heart ; and in my retrospect of vision I find all I saw falling into two categories which I think correspond to the Mid-world and World of Immortal Youth of the ancestors. My vision into the highest of these spheres was rare, and only once did consciousness for a moment follow vision and I seemed myself to be in the world I contemplated. At other times I was like one who cannot enter the gardens of a palace, but who gazes distantly through gates on their beauty, and sees people of a higher order than himself moving in a world enchanting to his eyes. I did see in some sphere interpenetrated with this beings in an ecstasy of radiance, colour and sound, lovers who seemed enraptured with their happiness, as they tell in old story of lovers on the plains of Moy Mell, and to me they seemed like some who had lived in Earth in ancient days and who now were in the happy world. And I saw, without being able to explain to myself their relation to that exalted humanity, beings such as the ancient poets described, a divine folk who I think never were human but were those spoken of as the Sidhe. I did not see enough to enable me to speak with any certainty about their life, and I do not know that it would serve any useful purpose to detail visions which remain bewildering to myself. Into the lowest of these two spheres I saw with more frequency, but was able to understand but little of what I saw. I will tell one or two visions out of many. I was drawn to meditate beside a deep pool amid woods. It was a place charged with psychic life, and was regarded with some awe by the people who lived near. As I gazed into the dark waters consciousness seemed to sink beneath them and I found myself in another world. It was more luminous than this, and I found one there who seemed like an

elemental king.   He was seated on a throne,
and I saw that a lustrous air rose up as from
a fountain beneath the seat and his breathing
of it gave him power.   The figure was of a
brilliant blue and gold opalescence, and the
breast, as with many of the higher beings, was
shining, and a golden light seemed to pervade
the whole body and to shine through its
silvery blueness.   The tribe he ruled were
smaller than himself, and these I saw descending on the right of the throne, their
shining dimmed to a kind of greyness, and
each one as it came before the throne bent
forward and pressed its lips upon the heart of
the king, and in an instant at the touch it
became flushed with life and it shot up plumed
and radiant, and there was a continuous
descent on one side of grey elementals and
on the other side a continuous ascent of
radiant figures, and I know not what it meant.
And at another time I saw one of these lesser
beings flying as a messenger out of the heart
of one greater, and I saw a return to the
heart and the vanishing of the lesser in the
greater, and I know not what it meant.
And at another time I was astonished, for I
saw rising out of deep water seven shining
and silvery figures, and three on one side and

three on another side and one beneath, they held uplifted hands on the hilt of a gigantic sword of quivering flame, and they waved that mighty sword in air and sank again beneath the waters. And after that seven others rose up and they held a great spear, and it they pointed skywards and sank below ; and after that arose two carrying a cauldron, and, when they had vanished, one solitary figure arose and it held in its hands a great and glittering stone ; and why these beautiful beings should bring forth the four precious symbols of the Tuatha de Danaan I do not know, for that Mid-world, as Usheen travelling to Tirnanoge saw, is full of strange and beautiful forms appearing and vanishing ever about the mystic adventurer, and there are to be seen many beings such as the bards told of : beings riding like Lir or Mananan upon winged steeds, or surrounded like Angus Oge with many-coloured birds, and why these images of beauty and mystery should be there I do not know, but they entered into the imagination of poets in the past and have entered into the imagination of others who are still living. I can only surmise that they were given the names of Mananan, Angus, Dana or Lir because they were mouthpieces of the bodiless deities and perhaps sitting on high thrones represented these at the Druidic mysteries, and when the mortal came to be made immortal they spoke to him each out of their peculiar wisdom. In myself as in others I know they awakened ecstasy. To one who lay on the mound which is called the Brugh on the Boyne a form like that the bards speak of Angus appeared, and it cried : "Can you not see me ? Can you not hear me ? I come from the Land of Immortal Youth." And I, though I could not be certain of speech, found the wild words flying up to my brain interpreting my own vision of the god, and it seemed to be crying to me : "Oh, see our sun is dawning for us, ever dawning, with ever youthful and triumphant voices. Your sun is but a smoky shadow : ours the ruddy and eternal glow. Your fire is far away, but ours within our hearts is ever living and through wood and wave is ever dawning on adoring eyes. My birds from purple fiery plumage shed the light of lights. Their kisses wake the love that never dies and leads through death to me. My love shall be in thine when love is sacrifice." I do not believe that either to myself or my friend were such words spoken, but the whole being is lifted up in vision and overmastered, and the words that came flying upward in consciousness perhaps represent our sudden harmony with a life which is beyond ourselves, we in our words interpreting the life of the spirit. Some interpret the spirit with sadness and some with joy, but in this country I think it will always cry out its wild and wondrous story of immortal youth and will lead its votaries to a heaven where they will be drunken with beauty. What is all this? Poetry or fantasy? It has visited thousands in all ages and lands, and from such visions have come all that is most beautiful in poetry or art. These forms inhabited Shelley's luminous cloudland, and they were the models in the Pheidian heart, and they have been with artist, poet and musician since the beginning of the world, and they will be with us until we grow into their beauty and learn from them how to fulfil human destiny, accomplishing our labour which is to make this world into the likeness of the Kingdom of Light.

EARTH

I THINK of earth as the floor of a cathedral
where altar and Presence are everywhere.
This reverence came to me as a boy listening
to the voice of birds one coloured evening in
summer, when suddenly birds and trees and
grass and tinted air and myself seemed but
one mood or companionship, and I felt a
certitude that the same spirit was in all. A
little breaking of the barriers and being would
mingle with being. Whitman writes of the
earth that it is rude and incomprehensible at
first. "But I swear to you," he cries, "that
there are divine things well hidden." Yet
they are not so concealed that the lover may
not discover them, and to the lover nature
reveals herself like a shy maiden who is
slowly drawn to one who adores her at a
distance, and who is first acknowledged by a
lifting of the veil, a long-remembered glance,
a glimmering smile, and at last comes speech

and the mingling of life with life. So the lover of Earth obtains his reward, and little by little the veil is lifted of an inexhaustible beauty and majesty. It may be he will be tranced in some spiritual communion, or will find his being overflowing into the being of the elements, or become aware that they are breathing their life into his own. Or Earth may become on an instant all faery to him, and earth and air resound with the music of its invisible people. Or the trees and rocks may waver before his eyes and become transparent, revealing what creatures were hidden from him by the curtain, and he will know as the ancients did of dryad and hama-dryad, of genii of wood and mountain. Or earth may suddenly blaze about him with supernatural light in some lonely spot amid the hills, and he will find he stands as the prophet in a place that is holy ground, and he may breathe the intoxicating exhalations as did the sibyls of old. Or his love may hurry him away in dream to share in deeper mysteries, and he may see the palace chambers of nature where the wise ones dwell in secret, looking out over the nations, breathing power into this man's heart or that man's brain, on any who appear to their vision to wear the colour of truth. So gradually the earth lover realises the golden world is all about him in imperishable beauty, and he may pass from the vision to the profounder beauty of being, and know an eternal love is within and around him, pressing upon him and sustaining with infinite tenderness his body, his soul and his spirit.

I have obscured the vision of that being by dilating too much on what was curious, but I desired to draw others to this meditation, if by reasoning it were possible to free the intellect from its own fetters, so that the imagination might go forth, as Blake says, " in uncurbed glory." So I stayed the vision which might have been art, or the ecstasy which might have been poetry, and asked of them rather to lead me back to the ancestral fountain from which they issued. I think by this meditation we can renew for ourselves the magic and beauty of Earth, and understand the meaning of things in the sacred books which had grown dim. We have so passed away from vital contact with divine powers that they have become for most names for the veriest abstractions, and those who read do not know that the Mighty Mother is that Earth on which they tread and whose holy substance they call common clay ; or that the Paraclete is the strength of our being, the power which binds atom to atom and Earth to Heaven : or that the Christos is the Magician of the Beautiful and that it is not only the Architect of the God-world but is that in us which sees beauty, creates beauty, and it is verily wisdom in us and is our deepest self ; or that the Father is the fountain of substance and power and wisdom, and that we could not lift an eyelash but that we have our being in Him. When we turn from books to living nature we begin to understand the ancient wisdom, and it is no longer an abstraction, for the Great Spirit whose home is in the vast becomes for us a moving glamour in the heavens, a dropping tenderness at twilight, a visionary light in the hills, a voice in the heart, the Earth underfoot becomes sacred, and the air we breathe is like wine poured out for us by some heavenly cupbearer.

As we grow intimate with earth we realise what sweet and august things await humanity when it goes back to that forgotten mother. Who would be ambitious, who would wish to fling a name like Caesar's in the air, if he saw what thrones and majesties awaited the heavenly adventurer? Who would hate if he could see beneath the husk of the body the spirit which is obscured and imprisoned there, and how it was brother to his own spirit and all were children of the King? Who would weary of nature or think it a solitude once the veil had been lifted for him, once he had seen that great glory? Would they not long all of them for the coming of that divine hour in the twilights of time, when out of rock, mountain, water, tree, bird, beast or man the seraph spirits of all that live shall emerge realising their kinship, and all together, fierce things made gentle, and timid things made bold, and small made great, shall return to the Father Being and be made one in Its infinitudes.

When we attain this vision nature will melt magically before our eyes, and powers that seem dreadful, things that seemed abhorrent in her, will reveal themselves as brothers and allies. Until then she is unmoved by our conflicts and will carry on her ceaseless labours.

> No sign is made while empires pass.
> The flowers and stars are still His care,
> The constellations hid in grass,
> The golden miracles in air.

Life in an instant will be rent
When death is glittering, blind and wild,
The Heavenly Brooding is intent
To that last instant on Its child.

It breathes the glow in brain and heart.
Life is made magical.   Until
Body and spirit are apart
The Everlasting works Its will.

In that wild orchid that your feet
In their next falling shall destroy,
Minute and passionate and sweet,
The Mighty Master holds His joy.

Though the crushed jewels droop and fade
The Artist's labours will not cease,
And from the ruins shall be made
Some yet more lovely masterpiece.

THE END

Printed in Great Britain by R. & R. CLARK, LIMITED, *Edinburgh.*

WORKS BY W. B. YEATS
THE COLLECTED WORKS
Crown 8vo. 10s. 6d. net each.

LATER POEMS.

PLAYS IN PROSE AND VERSE.

PLAYS AND CONTROVERSIES.

ESSAYS.

EARLY POEMS AND STORIES.

AUTOBIOGRAPHIES : REVERIES OVER CHILD-
HOOD AND YOUTH, AND THE TREMBLING
OF THE VEIL. Illustrated.

RESPONSIBILITIES AND OTHER POEMS.
Crown 8vo. 4s. 6d. net.

THE WILD SWANS AT COOLE. Poems. Crown
8vo. 3s. 6d. net.

THE TOWER : A NEW VOLUME OF LYRICS.
Crown 8vo.

OEDIPUS REX : A PLAY. Crown 8vo.

OEDIPUS COLONEUS : A PLAY. Crown 8vo.

FOUR PLAYS FOR DANCERS. Illustrated by
EDMUND DULAC. Fcap. 4to. 5s. net.

THE PLAYER QUEEN. Globe 8vo. 1s. net.

STORIES OF RED HANRAHAN AND THE
SECRET ROSE. With Illustrations by NORAH
McGUINNESS. 8vo. 10s. 6d. net.

STORIES OF RED HANRAHAN ; THE SECRET
ROSE ; ROSA ALCHEMICA. Crown 8vo.
4s. 6d. net.

REVERIES OVER CHILDHOOD AND YOUTH.
Illustrated. Crown 8vo. 4s. 6d. net.

THE CUTTING OF AN AGATE. Essays.
Crown 8vo. 4s. 6d. net.

LONDON : MACMILLAN AND CO., LTD.

2

BY SEAN O'CASEY

TWO PLAYS: JUNO AND THE PAY-COCK; THE SHADOW OF A GUN-MAN. Crown 8vo. 7s. 6d. net.

" Mr. O'Casey does for the Dublin slums what J. M. Synge did for the peasants of the Western seaboard. . . . On the stage his plays produce an effect of anguished intensity that can only be paralleled in the novels of Dostoieffsky. . . . Mr. O'Casey differs from Dostoieffsky in the fact that he has humour. Fun and terror can seldom have been so mingled before."—*The Daily News*.

" With Mr. O'Casey we have a fresh, alert talent, which promises more for the Irish theatre than any one since Synge. . . . Both the plays are extremely well written. Mr. O'Casey's dialogue is extraordinarily varied and lively ; one rarely meets a modern play in which characters are so easily distinguishable by their speeches."—*The Guardian*.

JUNO AND THE PAYCOCK. *Caravan Library*. Fcap. 8vo. 3s. 6d. net.

THE PLOUGH AND THE STARS. A TRAGEDY IN FOUR ACTS. With a Portrait. Crown 8vo. 5s. net.

" Of its dramatic power, its masterly quality, there can be no doubt at all. The play grips ; its characters are alive ; its speech is that which comes from living people, and goes to the heart. It reveals a finished sense of what is essential, both in dialogue and situation. . . . It is difficult to record an honest impression of this work without seeming to forget proportion and restraint. Its rare quality is so conspicuous, and, in the author's circumstances, so amazing. But assuredly it may be said confidently that Ireland has produced no such dramatic talent since Synge."—*The Morning Post*.

LONDON : MACMILLAN AND CO., LTD.